Anxious to dig in to another one of Deb Burma's books,
to do within each session. I was torn between wanting to l
its flavor or to jump into the next session to gobble up m
not only to fill your own cup with God's Word but also for
drizzles into each topic. It's great for sharing in a group setting.
Bible verse in each session to store God's Word in your heart. Then, on top of that, each
session provides an activity to share with others or to just reflect on the lesson learned.
Now, that's not the end. I love trivia, and each session taught me a little tidbit of coffee
history or trivia. Finally, the recipes can be made for the group before they attend, thus
creating another layer to this complex-yet-oh-so-tasty book. There is something for
everyone in this book—but mostly the words pointing to the amazing abundance of
love God daily pours into our cups.

SHELLEY MOELLER, LWML Vice President of Gospel Outreach, 2013–2017

Honesty, encouragement, and biblical truth drip from this study. Grounded in the real-
ities of life, yet abundant in the richness of Scripture, this study is perfect for a moms'
group or a gathering of women. Each lesson includes questions for self-reflection and
tangible experiences that point to the sweet truths found in the Word. Through rich
coffee-shop metaphors, Deb provides a space to dwell in God's presence overflowing
with grace and love. You can picture, better yet—*taste*—the richness of God's goodness
poured out for you. Drink deep the love that Jesus has for you in this book. Time and
time again, you are reminded of the good gifts lavished on you through Jesus. Whether
you are running on empty, filled full, or someplace in the middle, this study will speak
words of truth and refreshment to your soul.

SARAH GREINER, PLI Communications Leader

Sip, Savor, and Drink Deeply is written in a way that seeks to meet the needs of many
different kinds of learners. As an educator within the church, I see great value in the
way Deb incorporates rich word pictures, deep discussion questions, hands-on activities, and tasty recipes while guiding women on a journey to dig deeper into God's Word
and to savor the abundant gifts of God's grace. While working through this Bible study,
either individually or within a group setting, women will be met where they are, challenged to renew their minds with the truth found in God's Word, and, most important,
grow in faith in our Lord and Savior, Jesus Christ. So go ahead and take a sip—and
savor God's overflowing grace!

STACEY HOLT, Director of Christian Education

I was excited to grab a cup of my favorite warm beverage and turn the pages of my Bible
with Deb. This is no surface-level study! Deb includes a wide variety of Scripture texts,
questions, and insights to dig deeper in every session. She cleverly includes fun and
relational discussion, recipes, and optional group activities to build community and to
weave reminders of God's Word into our lives and the days between study. Best of all,
every page constantly turns us toward our gracious Savior, who is our overflowing cup.

HEIDI GOEHMANN, Deaconess

ENDORSEMENTS

Deb Burma's *Sip, Savor, and Drink Deeply* refreshed my thirsting soul. Deb's writing is always down-to-earth, real, and authentic. Her latest book is filled to the brim with rich, compelling imagery that immediately grabbed my imagination. The Spirit-led integration and application of Scripture provided me with fresh and powerful insights that are deeply impacting my faith walk. I can hardly wait to share this Bible study with the women at my church. Thank you, Deb, for once again investing yourself so deeply and following your calling to bless us in our growth as Christian women.

LOIS BARTELL GIORDANO, encourager, mentor, Bible study leader, writer, educator, former Director of the Women's Leadership Institute at Concordia University Wisconsin

Deb Burma once again takes biblical truth and shares it with warmth, love, and a healthy dose of fun. This Bible study is great for both individual or group study and the perfect complement to a warm beverage and a quiet moment. Filled to the brim with promises from our Lord, this book provides more than just temporary comfort: it is steeped in the hope of our Savior, Jesus Christ. Readers of Burma's newest study will be reminded of the overflowing cup of grace given to them by their loving God.

LISA M. CLARK, writer of *Blessings and Prayers for Parents* and fan of a good caramel macchiato

I am delighted to recommend this latest study from Deb Burma, *Sip, Savor, and Drink Deeply*! Deb has a wonderful way of taking familiar coffee-shop imagery, connecting it to our daily lives, and pouring in the rich aroma and flavor of God's Word to assure us of our redeemed identity in Christ and His abundant, gracious provision so we can fully express the uniqueness with which He has made and gifted us. You will savor the richness of Scripture and the fullness of our hope in Christ. As an extra bonus of fun, you will learn a bit about coffee beverages and gain a few recipes too. This study is especially meant to be shared with a group and includes some great ideas for spreading the "aroma of Christ" through special gift and activity suggestions. Grab a cup, pull up a chair, and savor your time with Jesus alone and as you discuss with others. You'll be blessed and recharged!

DIANE BAHN, PLI Leadership Essentials Team and Coach; lover of Jesus, Bible study, and coffee

Deb is a master wordsmith, giving you amazing biblical analogies to deepen your faith and expand your understanding of Jesus' love for you! In a profound but practical way, she includes Scripture, stories, and special projects you can do individually or as a group. The recipes rock too! Your cup will definitely overflow as you read and study *Sip, Savor, and Drink Deeply*!

PAT FICK, Can-Do Missions Director, Concordia University Texas

A BIBLE STUDY FOR WOMEN

SIP, SAVOR and DRINK DEEPLY

DEB BURMA

RECEIVE GOD'S OVERFLOWING GIFTS

CONCORDIA PUBLISHING HOUSE · SAINT LOUIS

Dedicated to all my friends and loved ones who have met me for coffee.
I treasure the time we've gathered together around a cup!

OTHER BOOKS BY DEB BURMA

Beautiful Feet: A 30–Day Devotional Journey (and Retreat Kit)
Treasured: A 30–Day Devotional Journey (and Retreat Kit)
Stepping Out: To a Life on the Edge
Raising Godly Girls
A Chocolate Life Women's Devotional
Living a Chocolate Life: A Bible Study for Women

Copyright © 2017 by Concordia Publishing House
3558 S. Jefferson Avenue, St. Louis, MO 63118–3968
1–800–325–3040 · www.cph.org

Written by Deb Burma

Scripture quotations are from the ESV® Bible (The Holy Bible, English Standard Version®), copyright © 2001 by Crossway, a publishing ministry of Good News Publishers. Used by permission. All rights reserved.

Cover art: Shutterstock

Manufactured in the United States of America

1   2   3   4   5   6   7   8   9   10   26   25   24   23   22   21   20   19 · 18   17

Let's meet for coffee. I'm writing and you're reading, and if you'll grab a cup, I'll do the same! In a sense, we'll be "meeting"— gathering as friends in God—over a cup. We can even call it a *coffee break!* Yes, a *break.* A time to sit back for rest and refreshment from the rigors of life. And *coffee*—a mere beverage? Hardly. The term *coffee break* is enticing, even if a cup of java is not the drink of your choice. As we meet, maybe you'll enjoy a chai tea, a hot chocolate, or a flavored steamer.

When a friend invites you to meet for coffee, she really wants your company alongside her beverage. Whether you meet at a favorite coffee shop, bookstore, or café, the conversation and camaraderie you share can fill and refresh as much or more than what's in your cup.

The Lord invites you to meet *Him* for a break that's even better than a coffee break with a friend. He, too, really wants your company. The conversation He initiates in His Word and the camaraderie He provides in His presence are more filling than any other.

Just imagine what the Savior has in store for us each time we meet Him with our cup of coffee (or the like) and, more important, with our "cup"—our *self*—a vessel created and chosen by God, redeemed in Christ, and ready to be filled for His purpose.

Grab your favorite beverage, ask others to meet you with their beverages too, and then open the Scriptures expectantly! Drink deeply from God's Word, accompanied by this unique women's Bible study. During each session, you will examine your "cup" in the light of God's grace. Rejoice as you learn that your cup truly does overflow in Christ!

Before you begin, you should know that every session contains several special features:

COFFEE BREAK! Each session begins with a checklist, fun statements to select as they apply to you. (Many relate to the session topic as a small taste of what lies ahead.) Used in a group setting, this icebreaker exercise encourages members to open up to one another in little ways, which will foster friendships and encourage communication in larger, more significant ways. Used by individuals, the checklist sparks insight. Starting with the second session, "Coffee Break!" includes time to share an insight from the previous session.

MEMORY VERSE Next, you will focus on a theme verse. Encourage one another to commit these verses to memory, and take this moment to review the previous session's verse as a reminder.

TAKE A SIP! Scattered throughout the study, you will be asked to pause and ponder personal questions. If you are studying *Sip, Savor, and Drink Deeply* with a group, you'll benefit by first reading through each session on your own, pausing to *take a sip,* and reflecting on your thoughts and answers to these questions. When your group gathers, you may discuss these questions together.

HE FILLS YOUR CUP These questions lead you into God's Word, where He fills your cup as you drink deeply from Scripture. On your own or in your group, respond to questions and apply them to your life. Allow time for rich and reflective discussion. (See "He Fills Your Cup" Answers, beginning on page 113.)

FRESH-BREWED FUN FACT You'll also find bits of coffee history and trivia that apply to the sessions and often aid in illustration.

THE SAVIOR'S GRACE PLACE MENU Your Savior has a "menu" of sorts, filled with the very best of His abundant provision and served up to you. At the end of each session, you will receive a selection from this amazing menu by way of the description of a popular coffee shop beverage. Though we will explore them one at a time in the first six sessions, we will see by the seventh session that He has ordered the full menu for us. Our cups overflow with an endless supply of each item, poured out in abundance by His grace.

PRAYER I encourage you to begin your study time with prayer. Ask the Lord to guide and grow you through the Word, by the power of the Holy Spirit. I've also included a special prayer that you may use to wrap up each grace-filled, overflowing-cup session.

COFFEE SHOP RECIPE A special recipe is included with each session, connected to its theme and topic. As you make, bake, pour, or serve each delicious beverage or rich dessert, let *it* serve as a reminder that your cup truly does overflow with the riches of God in Christ, by His grace. Share a related bite-size taste of God's Word with those who indulge with you!

ESPRESSO YOURSELF! Continue the dialogue about the powerful topics in your Bible study while offering fun fellowship and a hands-on reason to bring even more women together. Several activities result in the creation of gifts, tangible ways to share God's Word and a message of His overflowing abundance with others. You may choose to "Espresso Yourself!" during or immediately following your Bible study time, or you may wish to set another place and time, especially if you invite others to join you.

Extend your cup to Him; He is filling it already. As you take your first sip, it is my prayer that **"the God of hope fill you with all joy and peace in believing, so that by the power of the Holy Spirit you may abound [overflow] in hope"** (Romans 15:13). Whether you sip strong coffee, savor steamy hot chocolate, or slurp a flavored steamer, you will be filled to the brim and beyond with God's Good News—overflowing with hope in Christ. Receive the outpouring of His grace, His joy, and His peace!

—DEB BURMA, AUTHOR

MY CUP: CLEANED OUT (MADE NEW!)

Coffee Break!

Check all that apply to you, and discuss as a group:

☐ I own a coffee cup with a funny or meaningful message. It says: _____

☐ I continue to sip from a stained or damaged cup because it has sentimental value or it's a favorite.

☐ I have been known to compare my cup with someone else's, believing hers looks better.

☐ Hot, iced, or frozen, I love the delicious blend of chocolate and coffee in a mmm . . . mocha!

☐ My cup, once stained and cracked, is cleaned out and made new! *(Intrigued? Read on . . .)*

Memory Verse: "If we confess our sins, He is faithful and just to forgive us our sins and to cleanse us from all unrighteousness." 1 John 1:9

YOUR GO-TO CUP

Do you have a favorite coffee cup? I have several. And I choose a particular cup based on my mood, my cravings, and whether I'll be grabbing my beverage to go. When I'm ready to curl under a blanket with a good book, I make a mocha in my ceramic cup with the message "Chocolate is the answer. Who cares what the question is?" When I'm headed out the door, en route to my favorite coffee shop, I may grab my grande metal mug so I can ask for a discounted refill. If I'm in a silly mood, I want lots of whip piled on my flavored latte, so I choose my widemouthed earthenware cup. When I'm feeling sentimental, I pick up my trusty old mug that's faded from wear and has permanent coffee stains. And when I'm feeling celebratory, I break out my delicate porcelain cup to sip some herbal tea. Maybe you can relate. And maybe you have a completely different kind of cup. But have you ever likened yourself to a cup?

TAKE A SIP! Pretend you're a coffee cup. What style best describes you? Colorful ceramic with a bold or fun message? Natural earthenware? Elegant porcelain? Trendy paper with a sleeve? Or sturdy metal with a snap-on lid? Why?

COMPARING CUPS

Interestingly, the Bible likens each of us to a cup of sorts—a vessel, a clay jar (2 Corinthians 4:7)—created and molded by God for His purposes, much as a potter fashions clay into a useful container (Isaiah 64:8). We're going to learn more about that later in this session, but for now, let's take a look at these cups to which we are likened.

We come in all shapes and sizes. Maybe our cup is dainty and delicate, or maybe it's strong and sturdy. We are breakable like porcelain and dentable like paper, foam, and metal. God created all things to be good and perfect, but we now live in a sin-stained world and show more than a few cracks, chips, lines, and dents from the wear and tear of our sinfulness.

Like our favorite cups, we have an outward appearance and we carry a message with it. We want the outside to appear at its best, and that's a good thing, provided the reason for our attention to appearance is to give glory to God as we live redeemed and reclaimed in Christ. Our first impression says something about us, and we want it to be good. However, as we wonder how others view us, we may become distracted or even consumed with the outside look of the cup. In our world, *image* is esteemed; others may define us by our appearance and our accomplishments. This may cause us to wrap our identity and our value around our physical attributes and abilities. We may even secretly compare our cup with others', only to find ourselves disappointed.

One of our friends is the dainty, porcelain type and we think, *I wish I were more like her, delicate, beautiful, and feminine.* Another woman reminds us of a sturdy mug with a message, and we reason, *If only I could be more like her, strong and practical, not afraid to speak my mind and share my faith.* Still another reminds us of the popular to go cup, and we pout, *I envy her; she is so sophisticated—a real today's woman. She grabs hers to go because she has important places to be!*

TAKE A SIP! When do you find yourself comparing cups with someone else? Have you mistakenly wrapped your identity or value around your cup's appearance to others? Discuss.

Perhaps the woman envied for her outer beauty feels ugly inside. Maybe the woman who appears strong and practical while speaking a bold message is actually misunderstood or misguided, attempting to compensate for inner weaknesses. Is the envied woman of today feeling disposable? Or maybe she's running on empty, finding her only energy from the caffeine in the cup. Maybe in some ways, our cups are a bit like theirs too.

In our attempt to appear polished to others, we cover up the cracks or chips: cracked and broken promises; chipped and damaged relationships. The lines and dents we smooth over are like the battle lines we've drawn in anger or bitterness. We've sustained the dents from damage we've done to ourselves or others have done to us. And the stains, visible only from the inside, indicate internal damage that sometimes even we can't detect. Sin permeates us. We patch up and fill in these blemishes for outward appearances, but the flaws remain. We scrub, polish, and smooth our outward appearance so we look flawless to others, while inside we are damaged goods.

CLEAN THE INSIDE OF THE CUP

During Jesus' ministry, as He taught about the kingdom of God, healed the sick, and reached out to lost people with His mercy and grace, He came up against the religious elite of the day—the Pharisees and religious leaders. They kept their many man-made laws, traditions, and religious observances to the point of perfection, vainly attempting to appear flawless and insisting upon this impossible level of obedience from all people under Jewish law. All the while, their own sinful pride, greed, and self-indulgence permeated them. Jesus called them on it! Jesus rightfully lambasted these leaders concerning their hypocrisy and false piety, as recorded in Matthew 23. During His seven "woes" to them, Jesus said,

"Woe to you, scribes and Pharisees, hypocrites! For you clean the outside of the cup and the plate, but inside they are full of greed and self-indulgence. You blind Pharisee! First clean the inside of the cup and the plate, that the outside also may be clean." (Matthew 23:25–26)

HE FILLS YOUR CUP

a. Take a closer look at the verses above. Based on the context of **Matthew 23** and what you've just learned about these religious leaders, what did Jesus mean when He told them to first clean the inside? How is it possible that the outside may then be clean?

b. Read **Mark 7:1–8**. How does this passage help you understand why Jesus would use the cup as a word picture in **Matthew 23** to reprove the religious leaders for their hypocrisy and false piety?

The Pharisees and religious leaders thought they were cleansed—made righteous with God—by their works. We may point fingers at these poor, misguided men, wondering how they dared consider themselves righteous by their religious observances and lording it over others who didn't live up to their level of false perfection. Then we cringe as we take a good look at the inside of our own cups and see our own vain attempts to appear perfect to others—even to attain a righteousness by our works. But true righteousness comes only by faith in Christ through the forgiveness of sins.

Jesus warned the Pharisees, "First clean the inside." But we are unable to clean the inside of our cup on our own. We cannot, by our own strength, heal the inner cracks, the chips and dents. We cannot remove the stains of sin that permeate us. But there is One who can and does.

Just before His arrest in the Garden of Gethsemane, Jesus cried out in anguish, falling on His face and praying, **"My Father, if it be possible, let this cup pass from Me; nevertheless, not as I will, but as You will"** (Matthew 26:39).

HE FILLS YOUR CUP

Look up **Matthew 26:39** (above) and **42,** reading the context surrounding these verses as time allows.

a. What kind of cup was Jesus referring to? What would passing this cup versus drinking it mean for Him? for you and me?

b. Jesus prays, **"Not as I will, but as You will"** (v. 39), and later, **"Your will be done"** (v. 42). Jesus' will conforms fully to the Father's will. He is fully God and, at the same time, fully man. How do you see that in His prayer to the Father?

God loved us so much that He sent His own Son to us in the midst of our sin (Romans 5:8). He chose us—stained, damaged, and broken. And He sent His spotless, flawless Son to drink the cup of wrath and suffering in our place. Jesus cleaned the inside of our cups! He took the punishment for our sins upon Himself, submitting to the Father's perfect will so we would be saved through His perfect sacrifice.

CLEANSED!

Jesus endured the torture of crucifixion and the agony of death on the cross, and He died and rose, victoriously defeating sin, death, and the devil for us so we would receive eternal life and salvation in Him. We are filled with faith by the power of the Holy Spirit to believe His promise that **"If we confess our sins, He is faithful and just to forgive us our sins and to cleanse us from all unrighteousness"** (1 John 1:9).

He is with you now and always. He knows your struggle with current sins. He knows you're struggling to believe that your cup can be clean. Oh sure, you know that He's cleansed you in the past, but this week you've created another chip, caused another scar, and done more damage. Even today, you find yourself consumed with envy or pride as you've once again compared your cup with another's, although you know you shouldn't. So go ahead. By the Holy Spirit's leading, confess your sins to God. He knows your feelings of inadequacy and thoughts of comparison. He is aware of each broken promise, every scarred relationship, and all the damage you've done. Hold out your stained, cracked cup to Him. He is faithful and just. He is all powerful to forgive you in Jesus Christ to remove your stains, cleanse, and heal you completely, from the inside out. Today. Now. In the midst of the sin in which you still struggle. You are stained and marred no longer, but cleansed and made new!

He who cleanses your cup enables you to seek the forgiveness of those you may have hurt in your brokenness. Instead of comparing your cup with others', by God's grace, you can view everyone with unique value and share His love with them.

Christ cleanses you by His blood, shed for you at the cross! Turn to **Psalm 51:1–12** and pray these words of King David, underlining words or phrases that stand out to you. Then, read again the memory verse for this session, **1 John 1:9**. Take a moment to confess specific sins quietly, bringing them to your Savior and trusting in the cleansing power of His forgiveness.

You are cleansed, made perfect, and presented to the Father spotless—flawless—in Christ, who covers you with His perfection. Can you believe it?! It's true! By the outpouring of God's grace—His free-flowing forgiveness—you are a new creation in Christ. **"Therefore, if anyone is in Christ, he is a new creation. The old has passed away; behold, the new has come"** (2 Corinthians 5:17)!

A CUP OF GOD'S CREATION

By the Savior's miraculous work in you and me, we are able to view ourselves differently, to see the truth of our identity: that we are all unique cups of God's creation, His chosen and redeemed children in Christ. We are His masterpieces, designed for the purposes He has prepared already for us.

HE FILLS YOUR CUP 4️

You have unique identity and value, not determined by outward appearance, abilities, or accomplishments. Consider how each of these verses helps to define your identity and reveal the measure of your worth. In your own words, summarize your identity and value, based on these combined verses.

Psalm 139:14   Romans 8:38–39
Ephesians 2:10   Jeremiah 31:3
1 John 3:1

a. Remember, the Bible likens each of us to a cup of sorts; we are created and molded by God, redeemed in Christ, and ready to be filled for His purpose. Read about the cup of God's creation that is YOU! What word pictures are used in these verses to describe you and His purpose for you?

Isaiah 64:8
2 Timothy 2:21
2 Corinthians 4:7

b. No longer distracted by or fixated on the outward image of our cup, we can focus instead on the treasure that dwells within us, by the power of the Holy Spirit. Read **2 Corinthians 4:7** again, this time adding **verses 5 and 6**. The apostle Paul speaks humbly of carrying the treasure of the Gospel—the forgiveness of sins through Jesus. What's significant about Paul referring to himself (and to us) as jars of clay?

TAKE A SIP! You are a unique cup of God's creation and you carry the Gospel message of Christ! If you could write your message on the side of a cup, what would it say?

Mocha Mercy and Grande Grace!

For chocolate lovers, the most inviting items on a coffee shop menu likely contain the word *mocha*. Mmm . . . mocha . . . chocolate richly blended with steamed or foamed milk and espresso, and topped with real whipped cream and a dusting of more chocolate. This treat is rich and lavish.

If "rich" and "lavish" aptly describe the taste sensation of a mocha, imagine what happens when we add "mercy" to the description of this delight: Mocha Mercy. And speaking of rich and lavish, **"In [Christ] we have . . . the forgiveness of our trespasses, according to the riches of His grace, which He lavished upon us"** (Ephesians 1:7–8). In God's rich, lavish grace, we receive His mercy—the forgiveness of our sins! And just as our mochas are made fresh to order every day, **"His mercies never come to an end; they are new every morning"** (Lamentations 3:22–23).

When your mocha is served in the largest to-go cup, it is called a grande. There's short, there's tall, and then there is grande. Envision God's supremely generous grace overflowing even the grande cup. **"The grace of our Lord overflowed for me with the faith and love that are in Christ Jesus"** (1 Timothy 1:14). This is the grace we don't deserve, but He pours it out anyway, and it's filled with the faith and love of our Savior, Jesus, whose blood was poured out for us at the cross. God's free gift of grace saves us and sustains us, no matter where we have been or what we have done. No great big sin you've committed, nor the substantial pain you've endured, is a match for the size of His Grande Grace given to you. In His rich and lavish mercy and grace, we are free from the grip of sin and the sting of death.

[**Fresh-Brewed Fun Fact:** Speaking of free, drinking coffee was an early American expression of freedom. Following the Boston Tea Party in 1773, when American colonists refused to pay Great Britain's exorbitant tea tax, Americans turned to coffee as their beverage of choice as a statement about the freedom for which they were fighting.]

We don't have to fight for our freedom from the sin that held us captive or from the pain that's been taxed upon us. God has given us victory over every sin and struggle, by the riches of His grace!

Picture the overflow of His lavish grace covering you completely so that others are drawn to it too. Listen as they say, "Is that a bit of Mocha Grande flowing down her face?! Now there's a woman covered in mercy and grace. Where did she receive it? I think I'd like some too!"

HE FILLS YOUR CUP 6

You are completely covered with the outpouring of God's mercy and grace! To read more about His great big Grande Grace, turn to **2 Corinthians 8:9**. In the most incredible exchange, which reveals the extent of God's grace-filled love for us, Jesus made a trade. In your own words, explain what He willingly traded, what it cost Him, and what you received as a result, by God's grace.

Prayer

Dear God, thank You for cleansing and healing my stained, cracked cup, according to Your rich, lavish grace, which overflows for me in Christ. I am covered completely by Your mercy and grace, and I pray that others may be drawn to You as I share Your Word of Gospel and Grace. Forgive me for comparing my cup with others', and help me to remember that I'm Your workmanship. Embolden me by Your Spirit to share the Gospel message I carry in my cup. In Jesus' name. Amen.

MMM . . . Mocha Mix

2 c. sugar

2 c. instant powdered milk

2 c. powdered nondairy creamer

1 c. cocoa

½ c. instant espresso granules

Mix all ingredients in a large bowl. Transfer to an airtight container to store. Pour steaming hot water into a cup and stir in 2 heaping tbsp. MMM . . . Mocha Mix. Top with whipped cream and a dusting of chocolate, and enjoy a mocha much like the rich, lavish kind you'll find at your favorite coffee shop!

Mocha Truffles

What could be richer than a MMM . . . Mocha? A sweet mocha truffle treat, served beside it!

Filling

2 packages (12 oz. each) semisweet or milk chocolate morsels

1 package (8 oz.) cream cheese, softened

3 tbsp. instant coffee or espresso granules dissolved in

2 tsp. water

Coating

1 package (12 oz.) semisweet chocolate morsels

½ package (12 oz.) white/vanilla candy coating

Melt 2 packages chocolate morsels in microwave or double boiler. Add cream cheese and dissolved coffee or espresso; mix well.

Chill until firm enough to shape. Shape into 1-inch balls and place on a waxed paper–lined cookie sheet. Chill for 1–2 hours or until firm. Melt 1 package chocolate morsels and white candy coating in microwave or double boiler, stirring until smooth. Dip balls of truffle filling in mixture and place on waxed paper until firm. If desired, melt *additional white candy coating* and drizzle over truffles.

ESPRESSO YOURSELF!

Message on a Cup or "Memory Mug"

Create uniquely crafted cups with the message of your choosing! Simply purchase:

- Plain ceramic mugs (white or light color)
- Oil-based Sharpie® paint marker pens (not regular Sharpie® pens)
- Nail polish remover and cotton swabs (for mistakes)
- Stencils or stickers to aid with drawing, if desired

Create your message anywhere you'd like on the cup using the oil-based Sharpie pens. Consider selecting a verse from this session that speaks of your identity, or choose a phrase that conveys the saving love of Christ. Or maybe you'll want to write the answer to your last "Take a Sip!" question. Choose an acronym, like **COFFEE** = **C**hrist **O**ffers **F**orgiveness **F**or **E**veryone **E**verywhere. Or make it a real "memory mug" and choose to write a favorite verse to commit to memory. If desired, add designs. Use stencils or stickers to aid with tracing letters or designs; simply remove the stickers when you're done.

Allow time for the marker paint to dry thoroughly. If you notice any mistakes, wipe them off with a cotton swab dipped in nail polish remover. Preheat oven to 350°. Bake your cup for 30 minutes so the paint will adhere permanently.

Create personalized cups as gifts, sharing a message of Christ's love and reaching beyond your Bible study group to people who could use some encouragement. Package powdered MMM . . . Mocha Mix (see recipe in this session) into individual servings and tuck into each cup along with a spoon and the devotion book *Sip, Savor, and Drink Deeply Devotions.*

NOTES

_____

_____

_____

_____

_____

_____

_____

_____

_____

_____

_____

_____

_____

_____

_____

_____

_____

_____

_____

_____

_____

MY CUP: POURED OUT (IN THE DAILY GRIND)

Coffee Break!
Check all that apply to you, and discuss as a group:

☐ My cup, once stained and cracked, is cleaned out and made new! (Share a snippet from the last session and have a memory-verse moment.)

☐ I drain _____ cups of coffee/tea daily!

☐ Sometimes my cup runs on empty in the daily grind.

☐ I know where I can go to receive a FREE refill!

☐ I love a latte! (Does that mean I have a latte love?!)

_⊥_ **Memory Verse**: "God's love has been poured into our ✝ hearts through the Holy Spirit who has been given to ✝ us." Romans 5:5

D R A I N E D

I walked through the door of the coffee shop feeling drained and depleted. I had hesitated to meet my friend for coffee that day since it added one more commitment to my already-full schedule, but there I was. My friend waved enthusiastically from across the room to let me know she had secured a table for the two of us. Once I'd received my pick-me-up latte, I plodded toward her, clutching my cup. I had barely sat down when I found myself unloading a laundry list of responsibilities, commitments, deadlines, and more onto my friend. As I heard myself rattling off my list, it was obvious even to me that my life was full to overflowing with good things, and I was not lacking for relationships or purpose, so how could I be running on empty? Why was I depleted and drained?

As you walked through the door today, was your cup bubbling over? Maybe. Or did you arrive feeling a bit drained, depleted, and even empty?

[**Fresh-Brewed Fun Fact:** Speaking of drained and empty, Americans drain a total of 400 million cups of coffee per day, on average!]

Although we meet for coffee around a cup filled to the brim with liquid treasure, we meet with a cup—a vessel—that is all too often running on empty. But that cup is cleansed from the inside out, as we learned in our last session. It is a cup that is perfected and made whole in Christ—a cup that contains the treasure of the Gospel, by the Holy Spirit's power.

So why is our cup "empty"? drained?

Consider for a moment how you describe yourself based on the many roles you have in relation to all the people in your life. Maybe you are a nurturer or caretaker, a mother, grandmother, wife, daughter. You may be the one who "holds down the fort." Perhaps you're a problem solver, boo-boo fixer, listener, or cheerleader. Maybe you're the go-to gal, the boss in charge, the head of a committee, or the volunteer. You are a taxi driver, an encourager, or a prayer warrior. Perhaps sometimes you're the teacher and other times you're the student. In someone's eyes, you may be a relationship specialist, a referee, or a role model. And maybe you find yourself fulfilling the function of entertainer, finder, fixer, or secret keeper. I could name more jobs, but now it's your turn.

TAKE A SIP! Write at least FIVE descriptive words (like those I just shared, but not limited to them) that help to define your many roles in relation to the people in your life.

1.   4.

2.   5.

3.

We meet for coffee with cups running on empty when we have poured ourselves out for everyone and everything on the lists we've just made. We pour ourselves out in our homes, at work, in our churches, schools, and communities, and in connection with every relationship and commitment within them. Day after day, we give (and we give!) all that we *can,* all that we *are,* and all that we *have.* We pour ourselves out in *the daily grind.*

Some days in the daily grind are just that: Daily. Routine. Busy, but manageable. Good. Then there are days in the daily grind that are difficult. Accidents happen. Hard times hit our families or our friends. Loved ones become ill. Relationships are strained. Friends or co-workers are in conflict. Heavy expectations and demands are placed on us at work and at home. Everyone "wants a piece of us" and we pour out all that we have for them. Again, and again, and again.

In the daily grind, have you thought or spoken words such as these?

"Lord, I want to listen to them . . ."

"I know I should help her . . ."

"I want to give where they have need . . ."

"I would like to follow through . . ."

"I want to fix what's broken . . ."

"I need to forgive . . . again . . ."

"But I am drained. Empty. Poured out. I don't think I can give, do, help, or fix one more thing."

TAKE A SIP! Share one or more ways in which you have poured yourself out in the daily grind for someone or something this week. What warning signals might you recognize that let you know you're running on empty, down to the last drop, desperately in need of a refill?

Seeking a Refill

Where will we look, as we hold out drained, empty cups, when we're seeking a refill? Will we look to the people and commitments into which we have poured ourselves, hoping they can fill us? We reason that God designed us to be relational, so maybe we seek a much-needed refill from someone significant—a boyfriend, a husband, or a best friend. Or maybe we attempt to receive a refuel through our volunteer work or career. Perhaps instead we fill our ꞔᴜᴘʙᴏᴀʀᴅꜱ ɪɴ ᴛʜᴇ ꜰᴏʀᴍ ᴏꜰ ᴏᴜʀ ꜰᴀᴠᴏʀɪᴛᴇ ᴘᴏꜱꜱᴇꜱꜱɪᴏɴꜱ.

We can share our concerns with someone who listens, prays for us, and at least partially understands. We can seek temporary solace at work when other parts of our life drain us. And we can attempt to alleviate our anxiety over an issue with the distraction of a new purchase. But what do we find, if we're honest? As vitally important as our relationships can and should be, as satisfying as the best career may be, as helpful as any of our possessions are sure to be, no one person and no combination of these things can meet our deepest physical, emotional, and spiritual needs.

We may even become frustrated and disappointed in our relationships when we ask a loved one to provide what he or she cannot. Even the dearest person does not possess the ability to fill our drained, depleted cup in the many ways that we need; the most reliable person will one day let us down, move away, or pass away. While it is true that our relationships are some of God's greatest blessings to us, in this broken world, they can also be some of the very reasons we are drained. (All this said, the Lord may give us a healthy refill *through* some of our relationships. We will focus on this in Session 5.)

We are disillusioned with our work when it does not provide the perfect fulfillment we thought it would. And our very favorite stuff? The latest treasure today is often in the trash tomorrow as the newer style, version, or technology catches our eye. Although we have sought all kinds of sources for a refill (some certain to satisfy, at least for the moment), we may still be parched and depleted in the long run.

TAKE A SIP! As positive as the possessions, position (work), and people may be to us, they alone cannot fill our cup. Recall a time when you were disappointed or disillusioned as you sought a complete refill from one of these "three *Ps*."

Oxygen

A friend recently returned home on a business flight. She'd half listened as the flight attendant began giving the usual instructions, including those concerning oxygen masks: "In the unlikely event of the loss of cabin air pressure, oxygen masks will automatically drop down from above your seats." But her ears perked up when she heard, "Put on your own oxygen mask before helping those around you." My friend, also the mother of a preschooler, envisioned flying with her young son and thought, *How selfish! We're supposed to take care of ourselves first?!* Then it hit her. These instructions were not promoting selfishness but prompting survival. If she were emptied of oxygen and passed out while attempting to help her little one, she could be of no use to him or anyone else.

When we are depleted and drained, we need to be refueled and refilled before we can be of help to the people around us.

So let me ask again: where will we look, as we hold out drained, empty cups, seeking a refill? We look to Jesus, our Savior. **"Seek the Lord and His strength; seek His presence continually"** (1 Chronicles 16:11). And how does He fill us? With His life breath—His "oxygen"!—by the power of the Holy Spirit, as He comes to us in His Word and in the Sacraments; as He hears our confessions and responds to our prayers; as He fills us with His pardon, His presence, and His power. Only when we are refilled in Him can we effectively help others and assist in filling them. Only then can we place our relationships, our work, and our possessions in their proper places, thankful for them, and thankful to the One who provides us with them. Forgiven in Christ for our faulty focus on the provision and not the Provider, by His grace we can **"set [our] minds on things that are above, not on things that are on earth"** (Colossians 3:2).

Receiving a Refill!

Remember the story I shared at the start of this session, recalling the coffee break with a friend when I was drained and depleted? God used my friend that day to gently remind me why I was running on empty even though my life was overflowing with good things. She challenged me to give my laundry list to God, to seek His lead, direction, and strength for each day and in every relationship and responsibility. You see, in my desire to pour myself out for others, I'd failed to receive a regular refill in His Word.

As we pour ourselves out day after day for the good of others, God refills and refuels us in every way needed, out of His great love for us. **"For I will satisfy the weary soul, and every languishing soul I will replenish"** (Jeremiah 31:25). Much as we picture a full coffeepot tipped over our cups, pouring out hot, aromatic liquid, so we can envision our loving Lord pouring out the fullness of His love into our hearts through the power of the Holy Spirit.

HE FILLS YOUR CUP

"God's love has been poured into our hearts through the Holy Spirit who has been given to us" (Romans 5:5). Create an illustration from this session's memory verse. How can you picture God's love pouring into your heart? Let the words of Romans 5:5 flow into the space below, accompanying your illustration. Add color, if you wish, as you continue to commit God's Word to memory, and share ideas and images with one another as you create.

We soak up God's Word, call upon Him in prayer, and receive His continual presence and power in Christ's body and blood. He refuels and renews us so we can again pour out the same love onto others. We don't need to worry that we will pour out more (or faster) than He pours into us because just as the "grind" is a daily one and we are continually being poured out, so we can be refilled daily.

TAKE A SIP! What changes can you make in your daily routine to find time with the Lord and receive a refill, learning from Him and growing in Him through personal devotion time? What tools will you use? Make a plan and bounce ideas back and forth with others. Maybe you'll gather a Bible, devotion book, journal, and mocha truffles in a basket. Place it near a favorite chair where you'll walk by with your steaming cup; it beckons you to draw near (James 4:8) and have a seat.

HE FILLS YOUR CUP 2

a. Take turns reading aloud the following verses. As you do, ask yourself, with what is God filling me and, therefore, enabling me to pour out onto others?

Isaiah 49:13	Isaiah 40:28–31
2 Corinthians 1:3–4	Ephesians 4:32
2 Corinthians 9:11	1 John 4:19
James 1:5	

b. Choose one of the verses above as you think of someone in your life who could use an outpouring of the very thing mentioned. Write out the verse along with the person's name, and tuck it in a personal place that will remind you regularly to pray and take action, following the Lord's lead.

c. Specifically, what are you in need of today as you pour yourself out, serving others in the daily grind? Continue to search the Scriptures in regard to your specific needs; seek His guidance and trust in His provision for every need as He works powerfully *through* the Word and *in* you.

The Lord pours out everything we seek, filling us with compassion for someone who needs a listening ear, giving us words of comfort to say to those who are hurting, and blessing us with a generous heart to share with someone in need. He infuses us with wisdom and knowledge that enable us to help where we can, to make difficult decisions, to fix what we are able, and to leave the rest in His hands. He provides us with strength to follow through with demanding tasks and expectations. He gives us the ability to forgive as He first forgave us, cleaning out our cup and making us brand-new in Christ! He enables us to love as He first loved us. Only our Creator can see what lies ahead and precisely what we will need in every situation. Trust that He will give you the direction, answers, and strength for each situation, equipping you according to His Word.

HE FILLS YOUR CUP **3**

How does God's promise in Philippians 4:19 speak to you regarding your needs? **"And my God will supply every need of yours according to His riches in glory in Christ Jesus."**

Because He supplies our every need in Christ, God does so much more in us and through us than we can possibly imagine, through the power of His Spirit poured into our weak, easily drained vessels.

HE FILLS YOUR CUP **4**

Open your Bible to **Ephesians 3:14–21**. Read aloud together the apostle Paul's prayer for spiritual strength.

a. How does **verse 16** partially parallel **Philippians 4:19** above? How is it different?

b. Read **verses 18–19** again. Mark in your Bible or write in the space below the words that stand out to you. Close your eyes and try to envision the limitless breadth, length, height, and depth of Christ's love for you. Discuss this thought: To know the love of Christ IS to be filled with the fullness of God! (See **Colossians 1:19**.)

c. **Ephesians 3:20** proclaims God's power at work within you. Consider all that you may ask of God. Now consider all that you're able to think or understand. God is able to do how much more than you ask or think? _____ _____ _____ What do you learn about the measure of God's provision and power in this verse?

A FREE Refill

Some coffee shops offer special deals to repeat customers who purchase a signature reusable cup and return again and again for free or discounted refills. (Perhaps you're one of them!) We return to the Father again and again, empty, poured out from the daily grind and ready for a refill—a FREE refill!

HE FILLS YOUR CUP 5

As you arrive for your refill, consider a few important things that may help you. Look up the applicable verses below as you read and take note of each important thing. Write the key words or concept of each verse. Discuss how knowing these important things may help you as you arrive for your next free refill.

Turn Your Cup Right Side Up! Ask for a teachable, open heart to receive every word of wisdom the Lord has for you today. Hold your cup under His steady stream of grace. **Psalm 25:5**

Drink Deeply and Sip Slowly! Sit in the Lord's presence and drink deeply of His Word as it flows into you. Bring it to your parched lips and allow your thirst to be quenched. Sip it slowly, savoring every taste before you swallow. With every *sip,* you are refreshed; with every *swallow,* warmed and invigorated. Every God-breathed word (2 Timothy 3:16) entices in new and exciting ways each time you read. **Psalm 81:10**

Receive Everything You Need! Begin your time in the Word with great expectations, embracing His promises. The Spirit's divine power works through the Word, miraculously filling you as you receive everything you need for life in His name! **2 Peter 1:3**

THE SAVIOR'S GRACE PLACE MENU

A Latte Love!

A Latte Love. Hot or iced, latte is a favorite on most coffee shop menus, and it's at the heart of The Savior's Grace Place Menu. Creamy and bold, with or without added flavor, my latte is loved . . . a lot. (Does that mean I have *a lot* of Latte Love?!) The Italian phrase *caffè latte* is translated literally "coffee and milk." To make a hot latte, a shot of espresso is poured into steamed milk and the two marbleize as they mix. A barista may double as a latte artist, creating a masterpiece in the foam as one is poured into the other.

God's Latte Love is poured into our hearts by the power of the Holy Spirit (Romans 5:5). He loves us . . . a lot. But maybe you don't feel loved or lovable. Perhaps the world has led you to believe you must earn God's love. Or maybe you've fallen for Satan's lies and think that God's love has limits.

Our Lord's love knows no limits and has no end. We cannot earn it and we don't deserve it, but He lavishes it on us anyway. While our feelings may betray us, God's perfect Word never will. There we read that He so loved us that He gave His Son (John 3:16), who poured out His life as a sacrifice for our sins, filled us with faith, and gave us eternal life.

We are God's creations, His masterpieces, created in Christ Jesus (Ephesians 2:10) according to His plan and His lavish love for us!

And this love enables us to pour out love onto others: **"May the Lord make you increase and abound in love for one another and for all"** (1 Thessalonians 3:12). By His grace, we can abound—overflow—in love for fellow believers . . . and for all. *All?* (Gulp!) Even the unlovely woman who shouts at us in the latte line at the coffee shop? The misguided people in our midst who reject Christ and may even mistreat us? The family whose culture and values are so different from ours? You and I are to love *all* of these? Yes, and this is possible only because He first loved us (1 John 4:19). The Gospel frees us and the Holy Spirit empowers us to share God's Latte Love—the same love He first poured into us.

HE FILLS YOUR CUP

You can read about God's agape love all across the pages of Scripture, but turn to the little Book of 1 John. In four brief chapters, you can count "love" over forty-five times, including the simplest but perhaps the most profound: **"God is love"** (1 John 4:16). Try this: using a red pencil or a pink highlighter, draw miniature hearts around every "love" written across the pages of 1 John. Step back and look at God's love, expressly stated to you over and over. Choose favorites to read aloud!

Prayer

Dear God, thank You for the full, rich refill I receive in Your Word. Strengthen me by the power of Your Spirit so that I may continue to pour myself out for the benefit of others. Help me to remember that I am Your masterpiece. Because of Your redeeming love for me in Christ, I can overflow in love for others. Lead me to pour out the same love You've poured into me. In Jesus' name. Amen.

Instant Vanilla Latte Mix

You'll instantly fall in latte love with this delicious alternative to your favorite coffee shop beverage!

1 c. nonfat dry milk powder

½ c. powdered nondairy creamer

⅓ c. instant espresso granules

⅓ c. sugar

¼ c. instant vanilla pudding mix (Substitute chocolate, pumpkin, or other pudding mix flavor as desired.)

In a blender, combine the milk powder, creamer, espresso granules, sugar, and pudding mix. Cover and blend until mixture is a fine powder. Store in an airtight container.

Latte Instructions

To prepare a hot latte, dissolve ¼ c. mix in ¾ c. steaming-hot water; stir well. To prepare an iced latte, dissolve ¼ c. mix in ¼ c. hot water; stir in ¼ c. cold water. Transfer to a blender; add ½ c. ice cubes. Cover and process until blended. Top hot or iced lattes with whipped cream, if desired.

ESPRESSO YOURSELF!

Today, you've received a refill, by God's grace, as you studied His Word. Your refill enables you to *pour out more!* With whom is God leading you to share His Latte Love, His comfort, forgiveness, and more? As a group, prayerfully consider individuals, families, or a community of people who could use a real pick-me-up. Create and deliver these fun gifts:

Latte Gift Mix in a Jar

Small lidded jars or airtight containers

Instant Vanilla Latte Mix (recipe above)

Gift tags

Instructions

Ribbon

Make batches of latte mix (each recipe yields almost 2½ c. powdered mix) based on the size of your gift jars/containers and how many you plan to make and take as gifts. Fill containers and secure lids. Create or purchase gift tags, adding a message such as "Jesus loves you a latte! Sending you a little latte mix with a latte love and prayers!" Attach instructions for mixing hot and iced lattes) and gift tags with decorative ribbon tied around the lid or container.

SIP, SAVOR, AND DRINK DEEPLY

MY CUP: DUMPED OUT (SPILLING THE BEANS)

Coffee Break!
Check all that apply to you, and discuss as a group:

☐ My cup is poured out in the daily grind but refilled fully and richly in God's Word. (Share a favorite insight from the last session, and enjoy a memory-verse moment too!)

☐ I've received a unique wake-up call in the form of
_____.

☐ I have dumped out a bad cup of coffee that was brewed from rancid-tasting beans.

☐ I've been served something that tasted totally different from what I thought I ordered.

☐ I love to order a "bottomless cup" of free refills poured in faster than I can drink!

−¦− **Memory Verse:** "But He said to me, 'My grace is ⁻¦⁻ ¦+ sufficient for you, for My power is made perfect in + weakness.' Therefore I will boast all the more gladly of my weaknesses, so that the power of Christ may rest upon me." 2 Corinthians 12:9

A WAKE-UP CALL

A little boy surprised his mother with an early morning wake-up call, bringing her a cup of coffee in bed. He had made it himself and waited with an eager smile to watch his mommy enjoy her coffee. Mother grimaced as she took her first sip. She had never tasted such a rancid cup of coffee. She wanted to dump it out but her son's eager smile prompted her to force it down. Wondering how he learned to brew a cup on his own, she inquired.

"It was easy, Mommy!" exclaimed the little boy in reply. "You know the coffee you keep in the fridge? I just scooped some into a cup of water and put it in the microwave!" Coffee in the fridge? Mother was confused until she remembered that she had placed used coffee grounds in the refrigerator months ago to absorb food odors. As you might expect, later that same day, she dumped the remaining old grounds from the fridge to ensure she wouldn't receive a rancid-cup wake-up call again!

[**Fresh-Brewed Fun Fact:** According to my local barista and other experts, air and moisture are a coffee bean's enemies; when either one reaches the inside of the bean, it starts to rot and therefore produces a rancid cup. Beans are best stored in dry, airtight containers; the freshest flavor is produced when they're ground just before they're brewed.]

Maybe it's time for us to receive a wake-up call of another kind. To pick up our cups and examine what's been poured in. To recognize rancid brew for what it is.

Do we need to "spill the beans"? I'm not suggesting we give away a secret. No, I am speaking of spilling out the stuff that fills our cups but shouldn't.

Because we so desperately long for satisfaction, we may hold out our cups to be filled with all sorts of worldly things we believe will satisfy. These are just some of the ways we may overstuff our lives or fill our lives with bitter beans:

1. **"Fill 'er up! And fill . . . and fill . . ."** Some things have such great appeal to us (like the names, descriptions, and aromas of our favorite flavored coffees) that we overfill on them . . . again and again. We fall for the lie that if something is good, more of it is better. We turn on the TV and within minutes, our minds are filled with

that message: more of this will make you happy; more of this can fill your cup. A quick commercial check during primetime TV provided me these "fill 'er up" deceptions: trendy new clothes, a credit card with unlimited purchasing power, a restaurant's cuisine, a new toy, a certain brand of beer, a vacation package, an Internet relationship, a club membership, and more.

So maybe we overshop, overspend, overeat, overconsume, overdo until our cup overflows with "stuff" that cannot truly satisfy. Some of it is tangible stuff and some is the stuff that could easily occupy all our time and energy if we allow it to. We overfill but never are satisfied. Most of the cup stuffings may not be bad for us, in and of themselves, but our overconsumption can turn them into something unhealthy indeed as they threaten to crowd out anything of greater or lasting value. When we've overstuffed our cups, we may have a diminished thirst for that which is truly satisfying. And we put ourselves in danger of making an idol of it.

TAKE A SIP! Ask yourself, what might cause my cup to be overstuffed?

---

2. **"Bad to the last drop."** Some things are just plain bad, and we know it. Succumbing to temptation, maybe we allow our cups to contain media and messages with questionable topics, damaging dialogue, and immoral or illegal implications that may be glamorized in the eyes of our world. Maybe we've held out our cups to harmful habits and addictive substances, or to unhealthy thoughts like worry or fear.

Yes, a portion of our bad beans often includes the combination of worry, anxiety, and fear. Before I've chosen the flavor of the day for my cup of liquid courage, I've already grabbed a colossal cup of anxiety and filled it with several pumps of apprehension stirred with foamed fear and topped with whipped-up concerns. Worst-case scenarios spill over from my cup brimming with worry. My heart races and I have the jitters long before I've taken my first sip of real coffee! Can you relate?

TAKE A SIP! Ask yourself, with what do I fill my mind and my body?

---

3. **"That's not what I ordered!"** Like the beverage thrust into our hands that tastes nothing like what we ordered, perhaps some things have been poured into our cups before we realize that they aren't what we expected. And now we find ourselves stuck in some bitter situations. Maybe they include unethical business connections we assumed to be legitimate, or an unscrupulous decision made on our behalf that now affects our professional or personal lives. What about the movie we were invited to watch, not knowing its content? Or the event we were invited to, not realizing what would take place during it? And now the damaging images, words, and events are burned on our brains.

TAKE A SIP! Ask yourself, what has flowed into my cup, catching me unawares?

Whether these things were once so appealing that we overfilled on them, or so tempting that we caved in to them, or so surprising after we let them in, unsuspecting, the truth is that we can allow ourselves to be completely consumed by them. Even if the bad beans no longer appeal as they once did, they may continue to have a grip on us. Maybe our cup still holds these things that have control over us.

Spilling the Beans

Our accuser, Satan, would have us think we cannot **"lay aside . . . [the] sin which clings so closely"** (Hebrews 12:1). He wants us to believe the lie that we'll be forever stuck with the current contents that threaten to consume us. Maybe we recognize that we need to "spill the beans," but we are weak and don't know where to begin. We're afraid that we will fail miserably and find ourselves stuck with even more of them. We may even scoop them up off the path of least resistance, feeling alone and powerless to dump them.

TAKE A SIP! In what ways do you need to spill the beans? Take a couple of minutes to write down your thoughts; if you feel comfortable, share with someone in your group.

But we are not alone, and we don't have to listen to Satan's lies. Our all-powerful Savior is with us, holding us close as we struggle with our bad bean brew. He never leaves us, nor does He give up on us, even when we are weak and even if we have failed miserably, again and again. **"No temptation has overtaken you that is not common to man. God is faithful, and He will not let you be tempted beyond your ability, but with the temptation He will also provide the way of escape, that you may be able to endure it"** (1 Corinthians 10:13).

Our faithful God will not let us "be tempted beyond [our]

ability." He loves us too much to let us drown in our bad bean brew. He forgives us in Christ Jesus every time we turn to Him with repentant hearts, sorry for the sour beans we have allowed in our cups. We may not be able to spill them on our own, but we trust that God will "provide the way of escape," perhaps through a Christian counselor, a pastor, or a trusted friend who will hold our hands or hold us accountable. The Lord will enable us to endure in times of temptation—to dump the bad bean brew. By His grace, we can spill the beans.

We can dump out the contents when they're not healthy or God pleasing, when they take up cup space where something so much better could be. As we seek God's strength, we can trust His wondrous work in us. He may even place someone in our lives who has sought similar help and conquered, by His grace. Recall, for example, my specific reference to worry. The Lord has led me to **"cast all [my] anxieties on Him"** (1 Peter 5:7), dumping my cup on Him and admitting my concerns to a friend who understands my struggle with worry because she's been there. Sometimes I scoop up the bad beans of worry once more. But God is gracious; He forgives me in Christ and enables me to spill those bad beans again. It hasn't been easy, but I know I'm not alone, and the free space in my cup for greater trust has been worth it. I look to God's Word, confident that Jesus has me firmly in His grip as He tells me, **"Do not be anxious"** (Matthew 6:25).

And what about those things that were not bad in and of themselves, but we overfilled on them? Again, the Lord works in wondrous ways, enabling us to "just say when." He will help us to recognize when we've had enough and how much is too much, enabling us to dump that good thing when it is consuming us in an unhealthy way.

HE FILLS YOUR CUP

Read **1 Corinthians 10:13** again. Revisit the ways in which you need to "spill the beans." Bring these struggles and sins before the Lord and seek His forgiveness. Pray for your Savior's strength to stand up under temptation, for bravery to dump the bad bean brew, and for a way of escape, to keep it from filling (or overstuffing) your cup again. Ask for the Lord's clear direction and courage to seek help from others when needed.

He accomplishes amazing feats in you and me through His Word and in answer to prayer, and through the influence and guidance of godly people around us who can provide the encouragement, accountability, and support that we may need to dump our cup or "just say when."

Motivation to Make a Change

As we take stock of what needs to go, let's examine the how and the why of our motivation to dump the bad beans and make a change in our lives. We can "just try harder" all we want, attempting to operate in our own strength. We can allow ourselves to remain self-focused, seeking immediate gratification but achieving only short-lived or nonexistent results. Or we can rest in the power of the Gospel, responding to God's purpose and plan for us and tapping into His strength for long-term success! We walk in His strength by the power of the Spirit; we find our motivation in Him, not in ourselves.

HE FILLS YOUR CUP 2

How can you begin to make a change, by God's grace, concerning what fills your cup? Receive wisdom and direction from God's Word in the following verses.

1 Chronicles 16:11

Psalm 18:32

Psalm 118:14

Psalm 119:105

Isaiah 30:21

Jeremiah 29:11

Ephesians 6:10–11

a. Beside each reference, write a key word or phrase from the verse.

b. Apply the truth from these combined verses to understand how and why you can spill the bad beans, by God's grace.

c. Consider how this change will honor God or impact someone near you.

His Power—My Weakness

The apostle Paul struggled with a specific area of weakness: a "thorn in the flesh." Maybe he battled a temptation or maybe he struggled with illness. Although we don't know what his thorn was, we can relate to Paul's struggle; in our sin, we, too, are weak.

HE FILLS YOUR CUP 3

Turn to **2 Corinthians 12:9–10**. What does God have to say about your weakness and His power? How can knowing this help as you consider your struggles with an overstuffed cup or bad bean brew?

HE FILLS YOUR CUP 4

Revisit some of the specific ways in which you may have overstuffed your cup or found it full of foul beans; then answer the following questions. How do the following verses speak to you as you address each question? Seeking your Savior's power in your weakness, how might you live out your answers to each question?

- "Fill 'er up! And fill and fill . . ." With what can you fill (and fill) your cup that truly satisfies and has eternal value? **Matthew 6:19–21**

- "Bad to the last drop!" What accountability can you seek to help you dump your cup, and what safeguards can you put in place to keep the bad beans out? **Psalm 119:37** and **1 Corinthians 6:12**

- "That's not what I ordered!" How can you be cautious about what fills your cup? How can you "do your homework" to be better prepared for what may come your way? **Proverbs 4:23**

Free Refill!

We talked about free refills as we wrapped up our last session too. Our Savior invites you and me for a free refill—to **"Be still, and know that [He is] God"** (Psalm 46:10), but oh, how we struggle to be still! We fail to take the much-needed coffee break with Jesus that can fill our cups like no other. Then we wonder why we're worn out and weary, struggling to spill the bad beans.

"Come to Me," our Savior says, **"and I will give you rest"** (Matthew 11:28). We drag our weary feet to the One who gives us true rest for our souls through His life-giving gift of forgiveness on the cross and in the empty tomb. Our cups are cleansed, dumped out, and ready for a refill. As we read and reflect upon His Word of truth, we are refreshed and filled anew with energy, strength, and direction for the days ahead, by power of the Holy Spirit.

He is the only one who knows our every need—the only one who can provide and give what we need, when we need it, and in the amount needed, even as He may use the *circumstances, people,* and *opportunities* in our lives to meet those needs (a small sip of our topics for future sessions). He ultimately provides for all of our needs as only He can. Consider this verse from Scripture: **"And my God will supply every need of yours according to His riches in glory in Christ Jesus"** (Philippians 4:19).

Why would we look anywhere else to quench our thirst? A friend recently told me, "You crave what you're feeding yourself." It's true. May we feed ourselves on God's Word of truth, that we may thirst for it even more, and lest we become tempted to gorge on the things of the world.

As I shared in Session 2, some coffee shops offer special deals to repeat customers who purchase a signature reusable cup and return for refills. We return to the Father again and again by reading His Word, in prayer, in worship, and at His Holy Table. With His help, we've dumped the bad beans and we're more than ready for His kind of refill!

HE FILLS YOUR CUP 5

As you arrive for your refill, there are a few more important things that can help you. (Revisit Session 2, "He Fills Your Cup 5," to recall the first few important things.) Look up the applicable verse and take note of each important thing. Write out the verses. How does it help you to know these important things as you arrive for your next free refill?

Bottomless Cup! The beauty of drinking in God's Word is that the more we consume, the more our cup is filled. Our Savior continually pours His love and grace into us. Our cups never run dry because His mercies are always flowing! In fact, our cups overflow, even as we are fully filled and drinking deeply. **1 Timothy 1:14**

Refill Station! The church service is the great refilling station. Like the coffee shop, where baristas are always brewing a fresh batch or creating a specialty drink to fill our empty cups, so it is with worship. At God's house, our cups are filled as we receive His Means of Grace in the Word—read and proclaimed—and in the Sacrament, as we receive Christ's body and blood for the forgiveness of our sins. Our cups overflow as we worship the Lord, our Maker and Redeemer; and as we sing hymns and songs, offering up our praise and thanks to Him. **Psalm 95:6**

Bonus Blessing! In addition to God's gifts received in worship, we are blessed with the fellowship of other Christians worshiping beside us. We trust that God works through our brothers and sisters in Christ as we meet together at the refill station. We are blessed to love and encourage one another as we walk together, growing in faith and continually pointing one another to Christ. **Hebrews 10:24–25**

THE SAVIOR'S GRACE
PLACE MENU

Perpetually Yours Peace!

"Perpetually Yours? What in the world is that?!" I asked my barista friend while staring at the menu. When she told me, I nearly jumped across the counter; I wanted to receive one for myself! A Perpetually Yours coffee shop treat brings the best chocolate and cherry syrups together for a special taste sensation, blending them with espresso, milk, and whipped cream for a frozen, iced, or hot latte. Trust me, after one amazing taste, you'll want to sip one *perpetually*! A few flavor blends may be equally delicious, but Perpetually Yours Peace, by its name, gives it the privilege of being placed on The Savior's Grace Place Menu as it speaks to something we all want to receive—it speaks to the peace that is ours in Christ!

As Jesus prepared His disciples for His imminent crucifixion and death, He spoke to them of peace. With the same words, He speaks to us today: **"Peace I leave with you; My peace I give to you. Not as the world gives do I give to you. Let not your hearts be troubled,**

neither let them be afraid" (John 14:27). His peace is perpetually ours, incomparably greater and wonderfully different from the "peace" the world attempts to offer but cannot deliver. Our Savior bridged the chasm that separated us in our sinfulness from our holy God. By Jesus' perfect sacrifice at the cross, He reconciled us to God, giving us real and lasting peace. Forgiven for the bad beans we've allowed in our cups and filled with faith by the power of the Holy Spirit, we receive eternal—perpetual—life in Him!

We come to our Savior daily, receiving an outpouring of His peace: **"Do not be anxious about anything, but in everything by prayer and supplication with thanksgiving let your requests be made known to God. And the peace of God, which surpasses all understanding, will guard your hearts and your minds in Christ Jesus"** (Philippians 4:6–7). Like the first disciples, we need not be troubled or afraid. With a heart of confidence and thanksgiving, we can bring every care and concern to Him, and He brings us peace that's beyond our comprehension, even as we can envision it as a protector standing guard over our hearts and minds. And Christ's peace is ours—now and perpetually!

HE FILLS YOUR CUP

Read **Philippians 4:6–7** again, this time marking words or phrases that stand out to you and discussing them. What should you be anxious about? Contrast that with what God tells you to pray about according to verse 6. What does that tell you about His care for even your smallest concerns? Envision **"casting all your anxieties on Him, because He cares for you"** (1 Peter 5:7) and receiving a trade! What does He give you in return?

Prayer

Jesus, please forgive me for the bad beans I've allowed in my life. Thank You for the salvation You gave me at the cross and for the strength You give me each day to spill those foul beans. I praise You for the outpouring of Your grace and peace upon me, reconciling me to God. Fill me daily and perpetually with Your peace! In Your name. Amen.

Perpetually Yours Chocolate-Cherry Coffee Cookies

If you think the name of this cookie is a mouthful, just wait until you have a mouth full of them! They're the perfect dipping cookies to complement a Perpetually Yours beverage or a piping-hot cup of coffee!

1 c. flour

¼ c. cocoa powder

1 tsp. baking powder

¼ tsp. salt

½ c. butter, softened

1 c. sugar

1 egg

1 tsp. instant coffee granules

1 tsp. vanilla extract

¼ c. miniature semisweet chocolate chips

¼ c. white chocolate chips

1 c. dried cherries

Preheat oven to 350°. Combine flour, cocoa powder, baking powder, and salt in bowl. Beat butter and sugar with electric mixer until light and fluffy; add egg, coffee granules, and vanilla, and beat until blended. Add flour mixture and stir until just combined. Stir in chips and cherries. Drop spoonfuls of dough onto ungreased baking sheet and bake 10–12 minutes. Enjoy!

ESPRESSO YOURSELF!

Vanilla Coffee Candle Decor

Whole coffee beans (Inquire at a local coffee shop; they may give away old beans.)

Vanilla votive candles

Widemouthed clear glass vases or jars

Ribbon

Old coffee beans are no longer fit for consumption, but they're great for decoration! (While the taste may be bitter, the aroma is still wonderful!) Gather the supplies listed above to create beautiful, aromatic candle decor. Fill the vase or jar partially full of coffee beans, then nestle a vanilla votive candle into the center, allowing part of the candle to sit above the bean base. Accent the outside of the vase or the rim of the jar with matching ribbon. (Vanilla Latte aroma fills the air as the candle burns!) "Espresso Yourself!" with this quick group project and consider giving some as gifts, accompanied by the *Sip, Savor, and Drink Deeply* devotional opened to "The Aroma of Christ" (page 56).

MY PORTION AND MY CUP

As we examined our "cups" in the first three sessions in the context of the Scriptures, we received refill after refill. And we've been exploring a portion of the Lord's rich provision by way of unique descriptions of popular coffee-shop beverages. He pours out His rich brew, filling and refilling us as only He can. We will continue to fill up on several selections from the countless offerings on this amazing menu. Our cups overflow with an endless supply of each item, poured out in abundance!

In the next three sessions, we're going to examine what fills our cups in another sense, too, as we consider:

What Is My Portion and My Cup?

"The Lord is my chosen portion and my cup; You hold my lot" (Psalm 16:5).

As the psalmist proclaims, God IS my portion. He holds and secures my lot and yours—our future inheritance in heaven. Envision the Lord holding your future inheritance; it is secure through Christ's death and resurrection. God pours out salvation and blessings; He fills your cup . . . with *Mocha Mercy* and *Grande Grace;* with *A Latte Love* and *Perpetually Yours Peace* . . . and more, as you'll soon see. He also assigns your portion and your cup.

When the Israelites entered the Promised Land, each tribe received an allotment—a "portion" of land as their inheritance, promised by God through Moses. **"Joshua took the whole land, according to all that the LORD had spoken to Moses. And Joshua gave it for an inheritance to Israel according to their tribal allotments"** (Joshua 11:23). **"Joshua apportioned the land to the people of Israel, to each his portion"** (Joshua 18:10). The portion was hand-chosen and given to each tribe. Similarly, my portion is *my allotment for my cup.*

My portion—all that fills my cup—is from His hand. *What does my portion look like today?* Ultimately, my portion is my future inheritance in heaven; the salvation and eternal life I receive by grace through faith in Christ. Today, too, I receive blessings from His hand. Each of us receives our own unique portion, blessings poured out upon us by our Father in heaven, the giver of every good and perfect gift (James 1:17).

In His wisdom, the Creator knows what is best for us, and He desires to give us His best. He is our sufficiency (2 Corinthians 3:5), and He uses the portion that fills our cups as He works in and through us to fulfill His perfect purposes. His plans for our lives are far greater than we could hope for. But sometimes our current portion does not appear as we had envisioned it would.

In the next three sessions, we're going to take a good look at our portion and all that it contains:

You and I are *Filled to the Brim* with our very own unique sets of **circumstances**. Some are not so savory, but God will use them for good. He has given us the capacity for *Full-Flavored* **relationships**, which are, again, unique to each of us. He has created in each of us a *Specialty Blend*—the perfect marbleized mixture of our personalities and gifts and talents to be used for the **opportunities** He has in store.

MY PORTION AND MY CUP: FILLED TO THE BRIM (CIRCUMSTANCES)

Coffee Break!

Check all that apply to you, and discuss as a group:

☐ In my Savior's strength, I can spill the bad beans, hold my cup under His steady stream of grace, and receive a refill. (Share a taste of the last session and have a memory-verse moment too.)

☐ I've carefully carried a cup "filled to the brim," only to have contents trickle down the sides anyway.

☐ I find joy in dipping biscotti or cookies or _____ (fill in the blank) in my hot java.

☐ I have been known to add a copious amount of sweet cream to my cup when its contents are a tad bitter.

☐ I enjoy the relaxing combination of coloring or faith journaling and sipping from my cup.

Memory Verse: "I came that [you] may have life and have it abundantly." John 10:10

FILLED TO THE BRIM

Two longtime friends met for coffee at their favorite shop. As they sat together, sharing their current circumstances and reminiscing about the past, they dipped biscotti into steaming cups, savoring crispy bites between sips and dips. The barista approached them with a carafe in each hand, generously offering refills. Chatting with the friends, she absentmindedly filled the first cup all the way to the brim before she realized what she had done. With a nervous giggle, she lifted the carafe and apologized for the near overflow, only to repeat the same steps as she filled the other cup. In response to the barista's second apology, the friends giggled good-naturedly, remarking that they dare not dip their next bites of biscotti or their cups would surely *runneth over!*

It's not difficult to envision a cup that's so full it's ready to run over. Level full, it cannot accommodate even one more drop, let alone a piece of biscotti or drop of cream. I think it's appropriate to say that when a cup is filled to the brim, it contains hot liquid treasure *in abundant measure.*

Whether we realize it or not, our cups are filled *in abundant measure* as we look at our lives and consider our current circumstances. What does our abundant portion look like?

Sometimes, when I hear the word *abundant* in the context of my life's circumstances, I may think in terms of quantity. I admit that my life is filled to the brim with an abundance of responsibilities and commitments. I look at the number of tasks I have to complete; I lament the overabundance of obstacles I have to climb around. I think my "portion" might require a bucket-sized cup!

The Abundant Life

Jesus has a different abundance for me and for you. In John 10:10, He said, **"I came that [you] may have life and have it abundantly."** He fills our cups to the brim. And He wants us to do so much more than merely exist in our circumstances—He wants us to thrive in them! Abundantly!

All too often, people misinterpret Christ's message of the abundant life and take it to mean financial or physical prosperity. While it's true that our material means are all part of God's provision, misguided messengers may proclaim that God wants us to have an abundant life defined by material prosperity and wealth. But this is the world's proclamation, not God's.

The world cries, "More!" More power and prestige, more accolades and awards, more financial fulfillment. Caving to the cravings of the world, we may chase after *one more thing*, thinking that "more" will provide the abundant life, only to find that there is always *one more thing* and we are NOT overflowing with the blessed abundance we'd hoped for or sought. Maybe our only lasting abundance comes in the form of stress and even debt as our focus is taken away from the real meaning of the abundant life.

TAKE A SIP! Imagine you're an on-the-street reporter and you're asking passersby what it means to enjoy "the abundant life." What kinds of responses might you receive? What do you think it means for a follower of Christ? Keep reading . . .

As I stated similarly when we dumped the bad beans in the last session, material prosperity is not bad in and of itself, but if we seek after it, looking for the abundant life in it and hoping it will provide lasting fulfillment, we are sure to be disappointed.

Jesus warned crowds of people against materialism on more than one occasion. The One who came to give the abundant life cautioned against the very things that life should *not* be about.

HE FILLS YOUR CUP

a. What does Jesus warn against in **Luke 12:15**? Specifically, what does He say life should not consist of?

b. Jesus talks about life and abundance in this verse and in **John 10:10**, read earlier. How do these two verses stand in sharp contrast to each other in regard to the focus and fulfillment of life?

c. The Lord provides another warning in **1 Timothy 6:10**. While He doesn't declare that money itself is a root of all kinds of evils, what does He say? In your own words, write about this root and the scary things that have happened to some people as a result.

d. How do the warnings found in **Luke 12:15** and **1 Timothy 6:10** speak to you personally as you consider your current circumstances and the abundance that fills your cup to the brim?

The abundant life of which Jesus speaks in John 10:10 is one of spiritual abundance. He forgives our sins and gives us life eternal—now and forever—through His death and resurrection. We are rich in faith; we are overflowing with the gifts of God, the fruits of the Holy Spirit (Galatians 5:22–23). We're given an overflowing measure of each and every one of The Savior's Grace Place Menu items, as shared at the end of each session.

Contentment in Circumstances

Years ago, I worked beside a joy-filled woman of faith who confided her family's financial struggles to me. She and her husband worked tirelessly to put food on the table, and they rarely had money left for nonessentials, but they kept a coin jar in the kitchen. As their small change accumulated, on rare occasions they would delight in one treat: a shared cup at the coffee shop. Content in her circumstances, she celebrated each day of life in a way that left an impact on me.

My co-worker showed me that our lives of spiritual abundance in Christ can overflow with contentment and gratitude in the midst of material abundance AND in the midst of need—in every single circumstance.

Turn to **Philippians 4:11–13**.

a. What connections do you make between material needs and contentment in these verses? Paul contrasts the situations he has lived through, describing them in three different ways in verse 12. In two columns, write these contrasting words or phrases.

b. What secret has Paul learned regarding his circumstances?

c. Consider these questions and discuss: Have you ever struggled with contentment in the midst of plenty? In times of discontent, who or what is the object of your focus? Are your eyes fixed on Christ, the provider of plenty and the source of your strength, or have they shifted to an object of His provision? Explain.

d. With a highlighter or colored pencil, cover the two-column list with "CONTENT IN CHRIST!" Discuss what this means for you in your specific circumstances as you look to Christ for strength.

The Savior covers us with His grace, forgiving us for our discontent and for our faulty focus on our material needs. In His strength, we can be content and grateful for all we have—and even for what we don't have—trusting in God's perfect provision and believing that in His wisdom, He may lovingly spare us from some earthly treasure we think we want. **"But godliness with contentment is great gain, for we brought nothing into the world, and we cannot take anything out of the world. But if we have food and clothing, with these we will be content"** (1 Timothy 6:6–8). Whether we live by meager means or bountiful boatloads (according to the world's definition of abundance), we are Filled to the Brim with contentment and with every good gift from God, given in abundant measure.

HE FILLS YOUR CUP

In these verses from the Psalms and the prophet Isaiah, we see the abundant measure of God's provision in so many ways. Beside each reference, make note of what God provides in abundance. Pause to personalize His provision, noting specific ways He has provided abundantly for you in each area. Then use your notes as the focus of a prayer of thanksgiving to your Provider.

Psalm 31:19   Psalm 78:25
Psalm 69:16   Isaiah 33:5–6
Psalm 69:13   Isaiah 55:7

Even as He pours out His abundance onto us and we drink deeply, He continues to offer more. Remember the bottomless cup? What greater abundance could we ask for or seek? We cannot begin to imagine all the incredible blessings God has in store for those who love Him: **"What no eye has seen, nor ear heard, nor the heart of man imagined, what God has prepared for those who love Him"** (1 Corinthians 2:9).

THE TASTE OF CIRCUMSTANCES

Are your current circumstances delicious and rich in flavor, or are they bitter and nasty, chewy and stout, like the dregs from a coffee maker with a leaky filter? Quite likely, you're tasting some of both, whether they're a part of your personal life, work life, community and church life, or beyond. Maybe as you consider your portion of the circumstances in your life right now, you're not thinking so much in terms of provision (plenty or need), but in terms of taste.

TAKE A SIP! Think of three circumstances in your life right now that are delicious, rich, and smooth in flavor. Jot a word or two about each of them here:

That sip was refreshing, right? It's a treat to rejoice in the delicious details, the rich moments, and the smooth circumstances of your life. But you'll soon see how you're called to respond in the troubled times that fill your cup as well.

Maybe some of the circumstances poured into your cup right now are bitter-tasting ones. You're sipping a cup of strife and sickness, from family battles and bad news to disappointing diagnoses and chronic pain. Or maybe you're sipping a cup of struggles and suffering, from professional or personal struggles to devastating losses or depression. Maybe all you can see is the impossibility of your situation, the unfairness of it, or the pain in it. It's difficult to recognize any blessing in some situations or comprehend how God could possibly use your pain for a purpose.

Staring into the murky, dark depths of our cups, it is tough to see anything clearly. But one day, as the Lord promises, we will see clearly and understand fully. **"For now we see in a mirror dimly, but then face to face. Now I know in part; then I shall know fully, even as I have been fully known"** (1 Corinthians 13:12). When this verse was written, a mirror was a piece of polished brass, as evidenced by many archaeological finds. It did not provide a clear or perfect image. In the same way, when our cups are Filled to the Brim and we peer into them in just the right light, we see only a limited reflection. Either "mirror" provides an effective illustration of our limited understanding and knowledge. Perhaps someday we will understand better than we do now; then again, maybe we won't come to such an understanding in this life. But one day—in eternity—when we peer into Jesus' face, we will know fully, even as He knows us fully now.

Meanwhile, what can we do in the midst of murky, dark days? By the power of the Holy Spirit, we can:

- **Trust the Lord,** believing that He will use this for good as He works in and through us for His purpose. **"And we know that for those who love God all things work together for good, for those who are called according to His purpose"** (Romans 8:28). He may even use our struggles in preparation for yet another purpose to which He is calling us.

  "Trust in the LORD with all your heart, and do not lean on your own understanding" (Proverbs 3:5). We cannot rest on our own lack of understanding; rather, we lean into God's strong arms on every dark day and in the midst of every tough circumstance. We surrender our situations to Him, relinquishing our control to His and resting in His arms. We are steadied by His strength. And trust is foundational to the thanks that follows and flows out of it.

- **Give Him thanks** in the midst of every circumstance, no matter the taste. **"Give thanks in all circumstances; for this is the will of God in Christ Jesus for you"** (1 Thessalonians 5:18). He is always worthy of our thanks and praise (Psalm 18:3).

Espresso Yourself! Actively express your thanks to God by keeping a gratitude journal. Start with the sample at the end of this session as you "Espresso Yourself!" and list every blessing you can think of! As you thank God, consider specific ways He may redeem the murky, dark days too. Open your journal every day, revisiting past entries and adding to the list. As you look back, you may be able to see with new clarity a purpose in your pain or difficulty.

TAKE A SIP! *Trust the Lord* and *give Him thanks*. Ponder these two responses we can have by the power of the Holy Spirit, and look at them in light of a circumstance you find yourself in today. Which is more difficult for you? Why?

Sweet Cream in a Bitter Cup

As God pours His grace into our lives, it's like a pure, sweet cream poured into the bitterest of coffee. Is the coffee still there? Of course. Will the bitterness of our circumstance remain in our lives, at least for a time? Quite often, yes. But what we taste has changed. By the power of the Holy Spirit working in and through us, we are able to see the same situations in light of God's grace for us in Christ Jesus, who drank the bitter cup of suffering for us, dying in our place to forgive our sins and fill us with faith and trust in Him. We drink our cups with a new recognition of God's love for us and His work in us, as He enables us to taste something significantly different.

HE FILLS YOUR CUP

Enjoy this taste of God's Word, filled with reminders of His sweet grace and His all-encompassing love for you in every circumstance of life! **REAP** rich benefits from your study of this passage:

Read **Romans 8:31–39**.

Examine the passage more closely. What did you learn?

Apply God's Word to life. How can you relate these truths to your life in specific ways today?

Pray! Respond to God's Word, using this passage as a guide. Ask Him to help you apply it to your life.

Half-Full or Half-Empty?

The optimist claims his cup is half-full; the pessimist insists his cup is half-empty. Which answer do we—followers of Christ—claim as we peer into our cups? Neither! Our cups are abundantly full. Our Savior has filled our cups to the brim and beyond, giving us the abundant life in our unique set of circumstances!

King David, a man after God's own heart (see **1 Samuel 13:14** and **Acts 13:22–23**) who loved the Lord and sought to do His will, was the great Israelite king from whose lineage Christ would be born. He was the man inspired by the Holy Spirit to write many of the Psalms; the warring king who conquered lands, leading God's chosen people into victory after victory and a time of unparalleled prosperity. But King David's life was also filled with difficulties, trials, and sufferings. Adversity and struggles filled many of his days, even in the midst of his popularity and prosperity. As we study his life in 1 and 2 Samuel, and as we read the psalms he penned, we see evidence of his many difficult circumstances. In part:

- King Saul was jealous of David and sought to take his life again and again. (For additional study, read **1 Samuel 18–27** to trace a lengthy trail as Saul pursued David, who spent much of this time in hiding or on the run.)

- David mourned the loss of his firstborn son following his sin of adultery with Bathsheba (2 Samuel 11–12).

- He suffered family tragedies when his son Amnon raped Amnon's half sister Tamar and was subsequently murdered by another of David's sons, Absalom (2 Samuel 13).

- David was forced to flee his own kingdom following Absalom's betrayal and attempt to forcibly take the crown (2 Samuel 15).

- Even as a youth, David fought against lions and bears . . . and a giant named Goliath (1 Samuel 17)!

Could David claim that his cup was, at times, half-empty? drained? These are fitting descriptions of the worldly appearance of

David's portion for his cup during these and other trials. Yet King David said of his life in the Lord, **"My cup overflows"** (Psalm 23:5).

In many places throughout the Psalms, David openly cried out to God in his distress, sharing his fears and his feelings with words like these: **"How long, O Lord? Will You forget me forever? How long will You hide Your face from me?"** (Psalm 13:1). In his next breath, he declared the truth of which he was certain: God had not forgotten him, nor had He hidden His face from David. King David proclaimed the truth despite his feelings: **"But I have trusted in Your steadfast love; my heart shall rejoice in Your salvation. I will sing to the Lord, because He has dealt bountifully with me"** (Psalm 13:5–6).

HE FILLS YOUR CUP

Maybe, like King David, you find yourself crying out to the Lord in anguish in the midst of your difficult circumstances. Give them to God. Pray with the psalmist. (Why not begin with **Psalm 13**?) Find hope and healing in the truth: God has not forgotten you. You can trust in your Savior's steadfast love, rejoicing in the salvation that's yours in Christ. He "has dealt bountifully" with you!

David's continual praises to His Lord and Savior, even in the midst of dreadful circumstances, revealed his close walk with God and the abundant spiritual life David received in Him. You and I have received the same! Like King David, we are Filled to the Brim and beyond! By God's grace, we can say with King David, **"My cup overflows"** (Psalm 23:5).

Java Joy

Always on a coffee shop menu, java is an international delight!

[**Fresh-Brewed Fun Fact:** Java is available in some form all around the world, yet it was named for one particular place. Coffees were traditionally named for their ports of origin, and the Indonesian island of Java became home to early coffee growers who cultivated and exported it. The name stuck and is now a nickname for coffee in its purest form.]

Ah, the simple pleasure of a straight-up cup of brewed java! No add-ins; no steamed milk or swirled flavor blends. Just a clean, bold taste. As we sit down to a cup, it's a simple pleasure and pure JOY, right? Java Joy, that is!

We may use the word *joy* to describe a time of simple pleasure, but to be in the Lord's presence is to be filled with straight-up, pure JOY. **"You make known to me the path of life; in Your presence there is fullness of joy; at Your right hand are pleasures forevermore"** (Psalm 16:11). We rejoice that He has made known to us the path of life through the death and resurrection of Jesus Christ, whose sacrifice paid for our sins. Joy in Jesus can be found all around the world, on every island and nation where the Good News of salvation in Christ is proclaimed and shared.

He fills us to overflowing with the fruit of joy (Galatians 5:22) that only He can produce in us. This joy is ours despite difficult circumstances and even when happiness eludes us. By His grace, we can persevere in hard times, trials, and troubles knowing the joy of the Lord is our strength (Nehemiah 8:10). Even when circumstances threaten to change the outlook of our day, by the Holy Spirit's work in our lives, we can arise and shout, **"This is the day that the LORD has made; let us rejoice and be glad in it"** (Psalm 118:24). Glad for another day of life; glad for all He has done for us; glad for His presence and power in every circumstance.

While we can travel the world to enjoy a cup of java, there is but one particular place where we find and receive pure joy—in the presence of our Lord and Savior. As we take a sip, we can rejoice as we remember the place of "pleasures forevermore." That's Java Joy!

HE FILLS YOUR CUP 6

Overflowing with joy, we can praise the Lord in shouts and in song, just like the psalmist! (See **Psalm 5:11**; **71:23**; and **95:1** for a sampling.) Have you shouted or sung His praises aloud lately? Even if you don't think you can carry a tune, go ahead and **"Make a joyful noise to the LORD"** (Psalm 98:4) in whatever ways you can! He is glorified as you praise Him for His presence, His protection, His salvation, and more. Many hymns and praise songs are written directly from the Psalms. Create your own tune or follow another's; then sing or shout the very psalms I've just shared.

Prayer

Lord God, I praise You for the abundant life You've given me in Christ. Help me to trust You and give You thanks in every circumstance. Continue to fill me with joy as I face circumstances each day, trusting Your joy is my strength. In Jesus' name. Amen.

Almond and Lemon Biscotti Dipped in White Chocolate

The bitter bite of lemon paired with the creamy, sweet taste of white chocolate makes this crispy, crunchy biscotti a JOY to dip in your java!

2 c. flour

¾ c. cornmeal

1½ tsp. baking powder

1 tsp. salt

1 c. sugar

3 eggs

3 tbsp. grated lemon zest (from 3–4 lemons)

¾ c. coarsely chopped whole almonds

12 oz. white chocolate chips

Preheat oven to 350°. Sift together flour, cornmeal, baking powder, and salt. In another bowl, whisk sugar and eggs, then mix in the lemon zest. Fold dry ingredients into egg mixture. Stir in the almonds. Let dough rest for 5 minutes. Turn dough onto floured surface and knead gently. Shape dough into a log and place on greased baking sheet; bake 30 minutes or until lightly browned. Cool completely. Slice the log diagonally into ½-inch slices. Place slices on baking sheet and bake an additional 15 minutes or until crispy. Cool completely on a wire rack. Carefully melt white chocolate chips until smooth and creamy (do not overheat). Dip half of each biscotti slice in chocolate and refrigerate until chocolate sets.

ESPRESSO YOURSELF!

Start a gratitude journal today, beginning right here! Give thanks to God through creative expression. The stacked cups on the following page provide a simple illustration of Psalm 23:5—**"My cup overflows."** Gather colored pencils or other faith journaling supplies. Start by writing the verse in or around the cups. Then, as overflowing drips and drops, record God's abundant provision (like His grace, peace, joy, and love, to start . . .) and all the blessings in your life that come to mind. Color, shade, or decorate the page however you'd like, offering prayers of thanks to God as you "Espresso Yourself!"

Enjoy this activity together, sharing creative ideas, and continue faith journaling as a group or alone. Select a notebook, journal, or journaling Bible. Look for blessings big and little as a daily exercise in thankfulness, then list them in your journal, adding Scripture, images, and artwork, if desired. Savor and celebrate these small morsels of blessing as you would a piece of crunchy, dipped-in-coffee biscotti!

You may also wish to use the stacked cups as a template to trace into a journal or onto the space provided in a journaling Bible. (Trace it near **Psalm 23** or another passage that speaks of God's overflowing, abundant provision, like **Romans 15:13** or **1 Timothy 1:14**.)

God may use this time of creative expression to guide you through a difficult circumstance as He helps you focus on His abundance and your blessings, and as He leads you to thank and praise Him for them!

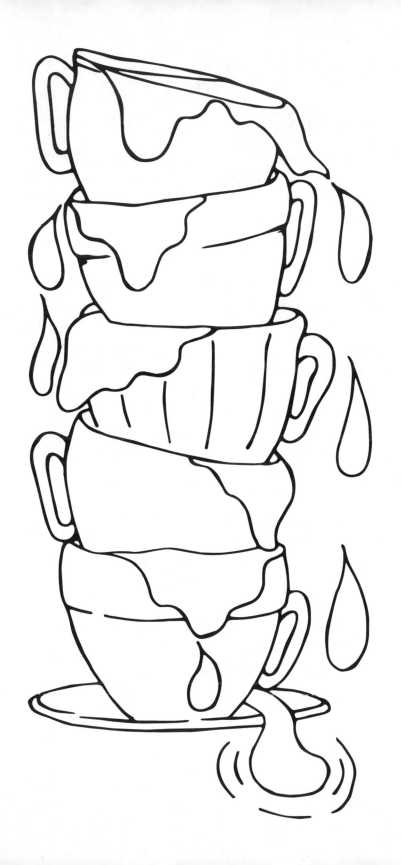

MY PORTION AND MY CUP: FULL-FLAVORED (RELATIONSHIPS)

Coffee Break!

Check all that apply to you, and discuss as a group:

☐ I am filled to the brim with the abundant life in Christ; He fills me with joy in the midst of every circumstance! (Share a bite-size portion from the last session and a memory-verse moment too.)

☐ I have a favorite coffee shop or café I visit so regularly, the people there know me by name.

☐ I sip my beloved hot beverage so slowly that I rarely drain my cup before it's cold. OR I drink deeply and request regular refills. (Circle one . . . or both, if your answer depends on the day.)

☐ Most often, I choose (circle one) speedy-quick espresso-based beverages OR slow brewed coffee.

☐ I like my coffee (or hot chocolate) steaming hot or iced/blended, but never lukewarm.

🕇 **Memory Verse:** "I am the vine; you are the branches. Whoever abides in Me and I in him, he it is that bears much fruit, for apart from Me you can do nothing." John 15:5

HE KNOWS YOUR NAME

I stepped inside my favorite coffee shop the other day and two familiar voices called out together from behind the counter,

"Deb!" A warmth flowed into me as if I'd already taken my first hot latte sip, and I thought, *They never forget me!* As I approached the counter, we began the friendly rapport we share each time I walk into their shop.

Sometimes I'm grabbing a cup to go; other times I'm meeting a friend. But that day, I arrived at my favorite coffee shop alone, ready to sit with my Savior for a time of devotion, writing, and prayer.

> ***TAKE A SIP!*** Do you have a place you like to go where you meet with your Savior for devotion time? If not, is there a place that comes to mind that you'd like to try? Share.

I've become what some would call a regular at this shop, and when I arrived that day, the baristas not only knew my name, but they also knew my favorite flavor blend, served up just the way I like it. "Let me guess, Deb: a halfsie again today? Half raspberry and half white chocolate; half skim and half whole milk; a half shot of espresso. Am I right?"

I laughed and nodded. We chatted a little while longer, then I headed to my table and opened my Bible. As I began to read, they delivered my drink. The side of the cup read, "We love Deb!" encircled in a big heart. Once again, a warmth flowed through me, this time as I pondered the expressions of love printed on a cup and written across the pages before me. I paused to pray, thanking God for the baristas' reminder that I am known. I am loved. I have a personal relationship with my Savior and with those He has placed in my life.

Relationship with the One Who Knows Your Name

As we continue to examine our portion for our cup, let's take a look at the abundance of its contents from another angle. Our cups are filled with the rich, Full-Flavored *relationship* we get to enjoy with the One who knows our names and expresses His love for us across the pages of His Word. God has called us into a saving relationship with Him by the Gospel—by His grace in Christ Jesus (2 Thessalonians 2:14).

Sure, my barista buddies call me by name, label my cup with love, and learn a little more about me each time we meet, but He knows me (and you) completely (Psalm 139:1–6) and loves us with an everlasting love (Jeremiah 31:3). He created each of us in His image (Genesis 1:27) and sent His Son to the cross to save us from our sins (1 Corinthians 15:3). He calls you and me His children (1 John 3:1–2), and He will *never forget us* (Isaiah 49:15).

HE FILLS YOUR CUP 1

You are known! You are loved! Reread the previous paragraph, this time pausing to look up each verse or passage. Take turns reading them aloud. As you do, remember that God is speaking directly to you. Which verse(s) do you most need to hear today? Why? Write out that verse or save it to your cell phone screen as a continual reminder to you.

Even better than seeing my name handwritten on the side of a cup is knowing my name is engraved on the palm of God's hand. And so is yours. **"I will not forget you. Behold, I have engraved you on the palms of My hands"** (Isaiah 49:15–16). He loves you and me! He knows our names.

While our Savior already knows us fully (1 Corinthians 13:12) and is with us always (Matthew 28:20), holding us close (Psalm 73:23), He desires that we draw near to Him as well. **"Let us then with confidence draw near to the throne of grace, that we may receive mercy and find grace to help in time of need"** (Hebrews 4:16). He listens as we communicate openly and honestly to Him in prayer. He understands us fully and He is always available. We can pour out our hearts to Him and trust that He will answer in His perfect way, will, and timing.

We grow in our faith relationship as we spend time with the Lord in His Word—as we allow the Holy Spirit to work in our hearts, increase our trust, and enable us to discern His will as we hear His voice.

The psalmist praises God, saying, **"You open Your hand; You satisfy the desire of every living thing"** (Psalm 145:16). Do we drink deeply of the abundance that flows from the Father as He opens His hand and pours out His divine grace and blessings? Or do we take only a sip here or there—just enough to moisten our lips—thinking that a drop of God's endless flow is all we need? Praise God, He continues to pour out His grace upon us whether we drink deeply or take just a sip. Ah, but there is nothing more thirst-quenching or filling than drinking deeply and receiving the satisfaction for our thirst that only He can provide.

HE FILLS YOUR CUP

Read Jesus' words in **John 7:37–38** for some thirst-quenching promises. By faith in Christ, what flows out of your heart? How do Jesus' words reveal His desire to have a growing faith relationship with you?

Jesus quenches our thirst for a Savior. In Baptism, God miraculously worked faith in our hearts by the power of the Holy Spirit, in water connected to His living Word. We are quenched, too, by the God-breathed words of Scripture that proclaim Christ's redeeming love and guide us every day of our lives. In Christ, we have already been filled with life-giving, forever-thirst-quenching living water. And we return to Him again and again for refills as we grow in our relationship with Him.

Full-Flavored

Rich, full-flavored, and fresh. That's coffee at its best. (The same could be said of hot chocolate and herbal tea!) We want to return for refills, don't we? Cup in hand, we sip and savor slowly so we won't miss the depth of flavor as we would if we hurriedly gulped it down.

Likewise, we return to our Savior for a refill. Bible in hand, will we sip and savor? We can gulp down God's Word quickly, but when we do, we miss the chance to taste the richness and depth of meaning in His words for us. Even when our time is limited, we can choose a few verses or a small passage to sip and then savor. As we meditate upon the words, we can write down our thoughts and respond to His rich, Full-Flavored message.

TAKE A SIP! How can each sip "stick with you" longer? Expand your gratitude journal to include your thoughts and meditations after reading God's Word. Like the mark of a coffee ring on paper, your responses jotted in a journal will leave a lasting imprint on you.

Study the Scriptures, finding, tasting, and extracting the blended-flavor details within them. *Blended-flavor details?* Consider how a combination of coffee or syrup flavors may be combined in your beverage, creating a unique blended flavor of its own. Upon further sips, however, you may be able to detect each distinct flavor within it. It's a multiple-taste sensation! Likewise (and so much better!), you and I receive multiple flavors from one verse or passage as the Holy Spirit leads us to greater understanding. The same passage may (a) convict us of our sin and prompt us to repentance; (b) show us our Savior; and even (c) move us to praise Him and respond with action. Other passages may teach us a portion of the history of God's people while also revealing a piece of God's will for us. Every word is brimming with His wisdom; we learn something new each time we read the same passage. When we sip slowly over each *blended-flavor detail,* we will often find that God's Word "sticks with us" throughout the day. The mouthfeel remains, and we find ourselves thirsting for even more as the Spirit works powerfully through every word.

Try the *blended-flavor details* study approach as you open God's Word today to receive a refill. Ask the Holy Spirit to lead you to greater understanding as you read. Begin with Jesus' words in **John 15:1–17**, as He teaches about the abiding relationship He chooses to have with us.

a. How are you convicted of your sin and prompted to repent?

b. What do you learn about your Savior?

c. Specifically, how are you moved to praise Him and to respond with action, by the Spirit's power?

Our faith relationship with Christ is the foundation upon which every other relationship grows. When we abide with the Savior, just as a branch is connected to the vine, we will be able to bear fruit and love others the same way the Savior loves us. Connected to Christ, growing in faith, enjoying a Full-Flavored relationship with Him, by His grace, we connect with others and grow in relationship with them too. (Isn't that exciting?!)

Speedy-Quick or Slow-Brewed? Every Other Relationship

[**Fresh-Brewed Fun Fact:** To pull a perfect shot of espresso, the technique of the barista and the conditions of the ingredients must be precise. Freshly roasted beans are ground not too coarse and not too fine *just* before they're packed at 30 pounds of pressure into a portafilter, through which the shot is pulled in no less than 20 seconds and no more than 35 seconds for optimal flavor.]

Speedy-quick. That's an espresso shot at its best. Well, to be precise, a perfect shot is pulled in about 25 seconds for optimal, intense flavor. That's speedy-quick, right? And even if the espresso is swirled with steamed milk, the entire process takes less than 2 minutes.

Slow-brewed. From the old-time percolator to the cold-brew coffee maker, these means of brewing take far more time but produce a rich, full flavor of their own.

What a contrast! From speedy-quick to slow-brewed methods, diverse coffee products are created, each uniquely delicious, yet somewhat similar too.

Let's have a little fun and liken these to the portion of our cups that includes all the diverse friendships and relationships in our lives. Some are slow-brewed, requiring years to develop their rich, full flavor. Others come into our lives like a speedy-quick espresso shot, and their influence—their flavor—is strong and powerful, perhaps for a specific purpose, and maybe for only one brief season of life, though maybe for more.

TAKE A SIP! Write the names of the first few people who come to mind as you think of those with whom you share slow-brewed friendships. Next, jot down a few of those with whom you have or had speedy-quick espresso friendships. Then share a bit about these with your group.

Every one of our relationships has a purpose and adds flavor to our lives. Some friends teach us valuable lessons while others learn from us. Some need our help and others reach out to us in our time of need. A few walk closely beside us through thick and thin. But all receive our love when we share it in Jesus' name. And all love in our earthly relationships is possible only because He first loved us and filled us with the capacity to love others. In our sin, however, sometimes we fail to speak or behave as we should; we neglect to communicate the love we've been given. Ephesians 4:29 says, "**Let** no corrupting talk come out of your mouths, but only such as is good for building up, as fits the occasion, that it may give grace to those who hear." If we're honest, we admit that "corrupting talk" sometimes spews out of our mouths speedy-quick in an angry or defensive reaction. Other times, it trickles out slowly because bitterness has been brewing a long while.

TAKE A SIP! Take stock of your closest relationships, and for each one, consider the kind of interactions you share. Ask yourself, is time together spent building up or tearing down? Are my words positive and encouraging, or are they filled with negativity, gossip, or discouragement?

Concerning every relationship that may be less than savory, lean on the Lord. Confess, repent, ask Him to forgive you, and be confident that He does, for Jesus' sake. Invest time and give priority to these relationships, seeking direction in God's Word and relying on His strength to do so. **"If possible, so far as it depends on you, live peaceably with all"** (Romans 12:18). Consider how you can do your part in mending what may be damaged or broken, giving grace even when it's undeserved, and steering your relationships toward a more positive place. *(However, let me say here that if there is emotional or physical abuse in any of your relationships, please seek outside help; you should not remain trapped in an abusive situation.)*

Think about the friend who is always ready to fill your cup with some fragrant blessed brew. She may or may not serve coffee when you meet, but you know she'll serve up some fitting words for the occasion while offering her listening ear. With the Lord's help, we can be this kind of friend, pouring a drink more refreshing than coffee, offering a flavor-rich cup that overflows with God's love and grace.

Vital Ingredients for a Rich, Full-Flavored Relationship

Desiring our cups to contain the fullest, richest flavor, with God's help, we can include the following vital ingredients in all of our relationships, and especially in our closest ones: *encouragement, accountability,* and *grace.*

HE FILLS YOUR CUP

Look up the supporting verses to the following three ingredients that contribute to the rich, full flavor God intended for relationships. As you do, apply God's guidance in these verses to one or more of your relationships. Prayerfully consider or discuss how you may work to enrich the flavor of that relationship in each area, with the help of God.

Encouragement Build up and stir up one another, pointing to Christ while providing edification, encouragement, and a listening ear.

1 Thessalonians 5:11
Hebrews 3:13
Hebrews 10:24

Accountability Provide a positive influence in each other's lives. With transparency and honesty, gently recognizing each other's sin instead of excusing it or looking the other way.

Luke 17:3
Galatians 6:1

Grace Extend God's grace to each other and pray for each other.

Colossians 3:13
James 5:16

For His Purpose

Open your eyes to *all* of the Full-Flavored relationships the Lord has brought into your life. With God's guidance, we have the privilege of pouring out His love in Christ onto others, whether or not we receive the same love in return. As we have opportunity to touch someone's life, we're reminded that every one of our slow-brewed and espresso-shot relationships is for *His purpose.* At the same time, we relinquish the selfish idea that our relationships are solely for our benefit. However, it's absolutely true that when we pour out blessings upon others, we often receive a "boomerang blessing" in return (our cup overflows too)!

HE FILLS YOUR CUP 5

In the verse below, Luke uses a word picture to describe what I called a "boomerang blessing" above. As you read **Luke 6:38** and envision giving to others, picture not only the blessing you receive in return but also God's measure of grace given to you. (For a reminder, return to **1 Timothy 1:14**.) How are they alike? Describe the "boomerang blessing" in your own words and share an example from your life.

"Give, and it will be given to you. Good measure, pressed down, shaken together, running over, will be put into your lap. For with the measure you use it will be measured back to you" (Luke 6:38).

Now *that's* a cup running over with *Full-Flavored* relationships!

A Fresh-Brewed Faith

"Fresh-Brewed and hot." Written all over a coffee shop menu, this describes almost every beverage option. Similar is the promise on the door of a convenience store: "A Fresh-Brewed pot every 30 minutes." Stepping into this store, we capture the aroma, knowing that the richest, fullest flavor will soon be ours because each cup is guaranteed fresh; there's nothing stale or lukewarm about it. And who likes their piping-hot beverage lukewarm?

Christ's words to the Church at Laodicea in the Book of Revelation warn us against a lukewarm faith: **"I know your works: you are neither cold nor hot. . . . So, because you are lukewarm, and neither hot nor cold, I will spit you out of My mouth"** (Revelation 3:15–16). These Christians had grown complacent and self-satisfied; they were apathetic about growing in faith or spreading the saving love of Christ.

In our sin, sometimes we turn lukewarm too, don't we? We fail to prioritize our relationship with God and with the people He places in our lives; we are self-focused and self-seeking. We neglect God's Word and worship; we fall short in our weak attempts to extend His love in Christ to others. We deserve to be "spit out," don't we? But God, in His mercy, gives us what we don't deserve: Forgiveness. Grace. Pardon for our selfishness and sin, paid by Christ's blood at the cross.

God's mercies are new every morning (Lamentations 3:22–23). He gives us a fresh start to each day of life as we live by faith in Jesus' name. As He leads us into His Word, He refreshes us with a vibrant faith, one that is once again fresh and packed with flavor for our Lord and His work in our lives.

Our faith helps define who we are, redeemed children of God in Christ (1 John 3:1) who are saved by grace through faith (Ephesians 2:8) and sure of our hope in Him, with firm conviction of our faith in the One we cannot see (Hebrews 11:1).

And our faith relationship with God in Christ is a springboard to action. By His grace, we share our Fresh-Brewed Faith with a world in need of a Savior, establishing and building meaningful relationships with those He places in our path.

HE FILLS YOUR CUP

Read **2 Corinthians 4:13** and **Acts 17:28**. As you do, picture the "springboard" of your faith relationship with the Lord. Because you believe, what springs forward as a result? By God's grace, what flows from you because of the faith within you? What difference does this make to the world around you?

Prayer

Father God, You know my name! I praise You for the Full-Flavored faith relationship that I have with You in Christ, my Savior. Lead me to love others as You love me and provide a purpose for all relationships in my life. Please forgive me for my lukewarm faith. Thank You for the fresh start I receive in my Savior. Lead me to share my Fresh-Brewed Faith with others. In Jesus' name. Amen.

Fruit-Filled Coffee Cake

This family-favorite recipe is packed with flavors, as it combines a buttermilk batter with a fruity filling and a cinnamon-sugar topping. Serve warm with your morning cup as you meet with your Savior or with other friends.

½ c. butter

1 c. sugar

2 eggs

2 c. flour

1 tsp. baking powder

1 tsp. baking soda

¼ tsp. salt

1 c. buttermilk

1 tsp. vanilla

1 can fruit pie filling (cherry, blueberry, peach, apricot, apple, or raspberry)

Ground cinnamon and sugar, for topping

Powdered-sugar glaze (optional)

Preheat oven to 350°. Cream together butter and sugar. Add eggs and beat well. Add flour, baking powder, baking soda, salt, buttermilk, and vanilla; beat about 2 minutes. Spread half of batter in greased/sprayed 9 x 13-inch pan. Spread fruit pie filling over batter in pan, then carefully pour second half of batter over filling, covering completely. Mix a small amount of cinnamon and sugar; sprinkle over top. Bake for 30 minutes. If desired, drizzle powdered sugar glaze (powdered sugar, milk, and vanilla) over top. Best served warm with Fresh-Brewed, full-flavored coffee!

ESPRESSO YOURSELF!

Coffee-Chocolate-Mint Lip Scrub and Spa Time

Before you take your next sip of coffee, enjoy a mini lip spa time together, where you'll make and take these lip treats as you celebrate friendships! As you moisten your lips with this flavor full lip scrub, think of the "blended-flavor details" study approach you learned in this session: First, enjoy the blended flavor of the exfoliating, moisturizing scrub, then detect each distinct flavor within: coffee, chocolate, AND mint! It's a multi-taste sensation!

½ c. + 2 tbsp. coconut oil

2 tbsp. ground coffee beans

1 tbsp. cocoa powder

2 tbsp. granulated sugar

10 drops peppermint essential oil

Small containers for sharing

Melt coconut oil in small bowl. Add ground coffee beans, cocoa powder, sugar, and peppermint essential oil, mixing until blended. Spoon into small, sealable containers. Ask others to join your group as you "Espresso Yourself!" lip spa style! Label containers, including instructions for use if giving as gifts.

Add Scripture tags: **"O Lord, open my lips, and my mouth will declare Your praise"** (Psalm 51:15). **"My lips will shout for joy, when I sing praises to You"** (Psalm 71:23).

To use: Apply to lips with fingers; massage into lips. Wipe off excess scrub with warm, moist cloth. Apply lip balm or lipstick as desired.

MY PORTION AND MY CUP: SPECIALTY BLEND (OPPORTUNITIES)

Coffee Break!
Check all that apply to you, and discuss as a group:

☐ My cup is filled with rich, full-flavored relationships—with my Savior and with those He has placed in my life. (Share insights gained from the last session and enjoy a memory-verse moment.)

☐ I rarely drink black coffee, but I delight in creamy, flavored lattes, cappuccinos, and the like!

☐ I prefer specialty blends over individual flavors when it comes to my favorite froufrou beverages.

☐ My espresso-based beverage serves as a caffeinated catalyst for the instant energy I need each day.

☐ I giggle over silly coffee slogans and made-up words, like *procaffeinate*—(n.) the tendency to not start anything until you've had a cup of coffee; and *depresso*—(n.) the feeling you get when you run out of coffee.

Memory Verse: "And God is able to make all grace abound to you, so that having all sufficiency in all things at all times, you may abound in every good work." 2 Corinthians 9:8

SPECIALTY BLEND

It begins with the shot of hot espresso. Or two. Or more! Then steamed milk is poured in, followed by your favorite combination of flavored syrups. Which will you choose? Chocolate and almond? Cinnamon, toffee, and caramel? French vanilla and hazelnut? The marbleized, swirled blend is unique to your preference. No two combinations are the same. Each is a Specialty Blend!

Similarly, God creates in us the perfect marbleized mixture of personality traits, abilities, and talents for the opportunities He has in store to fulfill His purpose in our lives for the benefit of others. No two people and no two portions are the same. Each is created uniquely according to His design, each with a Specialty Blend.

Maybe you think your Specialty Blend is lacking in taste or quality because others have lied to you, telling you it's bland or even distasteful, and convincing you to believe it too. Jesus knows your insecurities; He also knows the lies you've believed about yourself, and He forgives you. Jesus died and rose for you, and He speaks truth into your life, enabling you to throw out the lies. He says you are **"fearfully and wonderfully made"** (Psalm 139:14) and He continues His good work in you (Philippians 1:6).

HE FILLS YOUR CUP

Your Specialty Blend of traits and talents—every gift you possess—comes from the Lord. Read the following verses. Then, in your own words, share what they collectively teach you about God's provision and His purpose, as He works in and through you.

James 1:17	Ephesians 2:10
1 Peter 4:11	Philippians 2:13
2 Thessalonians 2:17	1 Peter 4:10–11

God's Gifts of Grace

Romans 12 provides us with a partial list of God's gifts (see also **1 Corinthians 12** and **Ephesians 4** for other lists)—a portion of the many and varied spiritual gifts He pours out on His people, by His grace. In a beautiful illustration, the apostle Paul compares each member of the Body of Christ to parts of the human body. Every Christian is given unique gifts for a special purpose, just as each part of our body is unique in purpose and function. All parts have a necessary function and work together. (See **Romans 12:4–5**.) While we share some of the same gifts, our differing gifts complement one another's beautifully as we serve side by side.

HE FILLS YOUR CUP 2

Read **Romans 12:6 8** and write out the gifts listed there. Your specific talents and abilities (which we'll soon study) may fall within these many broad gifts, given according to His grace. At first glance, which gift(s) do you recognize as your own, through which you may be called to an opportunity to serve?

Make a Move

Your opportunities, like your gifts, are also unique to you, allowing you to use the marbleized mixture of your abilities and strengths to serve a special purpose as no one else can. You will be blessed through every opportunity, and others will receive benefits and blessings through you. But guess what? You'll probably have to make a move to encounter these opportunities.

Making a move *toward* a new opportunity means moving *away* from something else. Does this mean a cross-country move? Maybe. Could it mean moving away from a comfort zone, as you step out of it and into an unfamiliar challenge or a new adventure? Even more likely.

TAKE A SIP! Look over the following "flavor" lists and **circle at least THREE abilities or talents** God has given to you or grown in you. Then **circle at least THREE personality traits** He has given you as well. (You may add to either flavor list as you think of a gift not listed.) Choosing one or two of each, prayerfully consider how God may be leading you to make a move using a combination of these gifts, blended together in a unique way at this time and for His purpose. Share and discuss.

Abilities or Talents

Bake/Cook

Communicate

Create

Encourage

Give Generously

Lead

Organize/Plan

Perform Athletically

Pray

Provide Care or Hospitality

Provide Support

Serve

Sing/Perform Musically

Speak

Teach

Write

Personality Traits

Adventurous

Artistic

Caring

Compassionate

Decisive

Dedicated

Efficient

Generous

Hardworking

Helpful

Insightful

Passionate

Patient

Resourceful

Selfless

Understanding

• Your Specialty Blend may allow you to serve someone in need. For example, if you're a great cook and you are passionate about encouraging others, maybe you can provide meals to new mothers or shut-ins, making personal deliveries and offering words of encouragement.

- It may enable you to help in a special way during a crisis. For instance, if you love to support the work of others and you're helpful and hardworking as you provide care in times of crisis, maybe you can join a team filling sandbags, boxing clothing for disaster relief, or helping victims in an emergency.

- Your blend might equip you to lead a new ministry or help with an existing one in a new way. For example, if you are dedicated to teaching, you communicate well, and you are adventurous when it comes to taking on leadership roles, perhaps you can lead a new midweek ministry, speak at an educational event, or serve on a teaching team.

You serve the Lord when you "make a move" to serve people who need their cups filled. And He is pouring His rich blend of mercy and grace into their cups through you. What you do well, do with excellence. And what you are still learning to do well, do with all your heart, trusting that God is glorified in your service as others see you giving everything you've got!

HE FILLS YOUR CUP

Read **Colossians 3:23–24**.

a. What kind of effort can you give, by God's grace, whatever you are doing?

b. Ultimately, whom do you serve, and what is your reward? How can knowing this impact your service?

c. How can these verses help when you are called to *difficult service* or when you work for someone who is *difficult to serve*?

Everyday Opportunities

Continue to think about your Specialty Blend and keep your eyes peeled for opportunities. What ones might you overlook because they don't stand out as such or even make your daily to-do list? Everyday opportunities might include making someone smile, offering up a prayer, or carrying someone's burden. Embrace everyday opportunities as part of God's plan. Trust that He will use them to prepare and train you for future opportunities that only He can see. In the meantime, remember that even in everyday moments, you are doing something as only you can, for the benefit and blessing of the people He places in your life:

• As you do your job and your co-workers see you give 100 percent, working with integrity and honesty,

• As you raise your family, performing tedious tasks for them with a cheerful heart,

• As you volunteer at a shelter, a nursing home, or a school to assist an overworked staff,

• As you use your creativity, your artistic skills, or your writing talents to brighten someone's day,

• As you share your musical gift, your technology expertise, or your athletic ability for the benefit of others, and

• As you give your time and energy to impact someone near you or the world around you!

Something Big

My friend Elizabeth enjoys a weekly devotional date with her Savior at her favorite coffee shop. As she sips hot chocolate, she savors time with God in His Word and in prayer; she reflects on her life in Christ and writes devotions. One week, she wrote, "As I headed to the coffee shop this week, I couldn't get my mind off of the desire to do more. I'd been lamenting about it the week before because I'm passionate about people who need to know the Lord and those who need to be encouraged in Him. All I could think was, *I want to do something BIG.*" As Elizabeth read her study for the day, she completed an exercise where she read Scripture and then recorded what she could do, by God's grace, if she was to live according to that truth. Following the exercise in God's Word, she wrote, "He reminded me to be content in all circumstances (Philippians 4:11). Even though *what* I do may not seem BIG, God has BIG plans, and I may never know how He will use the seemingly small things I do to make the BIG impact that He intended. The same is true for you. Maybe you are a mother figure to someone who doesn't feel loved or accepted by others. You are a sister to those who work with you, who could use your support and the example of your faith. You are an encourager to those who need to know they are valued. You bring Jesus to those who need to know Him. You are His child whom He loves very much."

TAKE A SIP! Ask the Lord to open your eyes to see those near you who are wandering around, holding empty cups and longing to have them filled. Take a good look at what God is already doing, and join Him in your unique way as He leads you, according to His grace.

As people witness your love in action, they will know the love of Christ because He lives in you (Colossians 1:27)—because He works in you: **"It is God who works in you, both to will and to work for His good pleasure"** (Philippians 2:13). All that you are able to do flows forward out of all He has done for you and in you, by His grace that overflows for you in Christ Jesus (1 Timothy 1:14)!

Abounding in Grace!
In **2 Corinthians 9**, Paul speaks of the **"ministry for the saints"** (v. 1), a relief fund for the destitute Christians in Judea who had

been hit by a widespread famine. Paul commends the first readers of his letter for their zeal in this ministry of giving. He also writes to encourage them to follow through with their generosity, so that their love in action would continue to be an effective example to others. He encourages us in the same way, beginning with a beautiful reminder of God's generous, abundant provision for us!

HE FILLS YOUR CUP

Envision God pouring generously into your cup the perfect "blend" to equip you for the opportunities He has in store! As you do, read **2 Corinthians 9:8** below, circling every "all" and underlining the word that follows each "all." Place a heart around each "abound." As a creative expression, sketch a simple cup; then write the word *ALL* in abundant-sized letters, completely filling the cup. Next, add the underlined words to the cup, using smaller letters to fit them (in any direction) inside "ALL." Finally, write "good work" several times, as if the phrase is flowing out of the cup in every direction, or write your unique opportunities (past, present, and potential future) in place of each "good work"; color, if desired. Describe your creative expression of God's abundant provision and what you're able to do as a result.

"And God is able to make all grace abound to you, so that having all sufficiency in all things at all times, you may abound in every good work." (2 Corinthians 9:8)

We trust that God will fill us beyond measure with His perfect portion for each of us, that we may not only do His good work, but *abound* in it! We have the blessed assurance of this in Christ Jesus, by His grace.

HE FILLS YOUR CUP

Paul continues this portion of his letter with further reminders of God's grace-filled provision, true for the believers in Corinth and equally true for you in your service today: **"You will be enriched in every way to be generous in every way. . . . For the ministry of this service is not only supplying the needs of the saints [believers] but is also overflowing in many thanksgivings to God"** (2 Corinthians 9:11–12).

With what are you enriched? For what purpose? As you give and serve generously, how can the ministry of your service create a twofold blessing for those you serve, according to these verses?

THE SAVIOR'S GRACE PLACE MENU

Espresso Energy!

Espresso means "fast coffee." A must-have on The Savior's Grace Place Menu, it's also the main ingredient in several other drinks, like flavored lattes, cappuccinos, and every kind of specialty-blended beverage. As you read in the last "Fresh-Brewed Fun Fact," espresso is created when steaming-hot water is forced under pressure through freshly roasted, firmly packed, ground arabica beans. A shot is "pulled" in approximately 25 seconds, producing a richly concentrated cup. And every shot of "fast coffee" provides intense flavor and instant energy. (You can imagine, then, the flavor and energy packed into a triple-shot latte!)

[**Fresh-Brewed Fun Fact:** According to Gallup,

research studies continue to report health benefits of consuming caffeine in moderation. It is linked to an increase in concentration and memory, and it may reduce the risk of several diseases.]

Most days, you and I could use a little instant energy and increased concentration, couldn't we? And our espresso serves as a caffeinated catalyst for it, especially if a typical day is *firmly packed with countless commitments*, or if we've been *freshly roasted* in the heat of difficulties. So maybe we place our confidence in the caffeine to give us what we need to face the day; to be energized for action or alert to the **opportunities** that may come our way as we work and as we serve.

I confess I've grabbed an espresso-to-go, thinking, *This is just what I need.* Soon, my pulse races; my mind and body are alert and ready for action. Then, before I know it, I'm *forced under pressure* to make decisions. Overflowing with energy, I may have a ready answer, but will it be a wise one? I'm reminded of a silly slogan on the wall of a coffee shop: "Drink Coffee. Do foolish things faster and with more energy!" Ouch! How easily I make foolish decisions when I fail to let God give me what I need to face the day (and I do it even faster after an espresso).

TAKE A SIP! Have you grabbed your caffeine-in-a-cup, hoping to receive from it the confidence to face the day or the energy for the opportunities that await? It can be helpful, to a point. Have you also found yourself making a foolish decision—even faster—when you've failed to let God give you what you need?

Praise God, I can approach His throne of grace with confidence (Hebrews 4:16) as I confess my failure. There, I receive the forgiveness that was won for me at Christ's cross. In my Savior,

I receive *everything* I need, from the Specialty Blend of traits and talents to the strength and energy to use them, and all as I face the next decision and the next day's work.

In the Savior's strength, the apostle Paul worked tirelessly to spread the saving love of Christ. As he shared the Gospel, he exclaimed, **"For this I toil, struggling with all His energy that He powerfully works within me"** (Colossians 1:29). God's Word has an energizing effect on us. Far better and longer lasting than a triple-shot latte, the Holy Spirit fills and empowers us with extraordinary energy to spread Christ's love as we work and as we serve. We may still grab an espresso-to-go, but we place our confidence in the Lord, who gives us exactly what we need for each opportunity He places in our path.

HE FILLS YOUR CUP 6

Let God give you what you need to face the day.

a. Read **1 Peter 3:15** and **James 1:5**. How can you be prepared with a *ready answer* that's also a wise one?

b. Combining your God-given gifts with His energy and strength, you can spread the saving love of Christ in the middle of your workday and as you serve others in His name. In these and other settings, how can you know that He powerfully works His energy within you? (See **Colossians 1:29** above and revisit, once again, **Philippians 2:13**.)

Prayer

Father God, I praise You, for I am fearfully and wonderfully made, created with a Specialty Blend of gifts so that I may serve You by serving others. Open my eyes to the opportunities before me. Forgive me, Lord Jesus, for placing my confidence in anything other than You. Work Your energy powerfully within me as I serve and as I share Your saving love. In Your name. Amen.

Espresso-Chocolate Chip Scones with Coffee Glaze

Look no further for a delicious source of energy, served "on the side" of your cup! Espresso coffee flavor blended with chocolate chips and cream creates a carbohydrate- and caffeine-lover's dream!

1¾ c. flour, plus more for dusting

¼ c. sugar

1 tbsp. plus ½ tsp. baking powder

½ tsp. salt

6 tbsp. (¾ stick) chilled butter, cut into small pieces

1 tbsp. instant espresso powder

1 tsp. hot water

1 c. heavy cream

²/₃ c. miniature semisweet chocolate chips

2 tbsp. butter

1–1½ c. powdered sugar

2 tbsp. strong freshly brewed coffee

1 tsp. vanilla

Preheat oven to 375°. Combine 1¾ c. flour, sugar, baking powder, and salt in a bowl. Cut in chilled butter until the mixture resembles coarse crumbs. Meanwhile, in a small bowl, combine espresso powder with hot water. Whisk in cream. Stir into dry ingredients just until moistened. Fold in chocolate chips. Turn onto a floured surface; knead gently, then pat into a circle, about 1 inch thick. Cut dough into wedges and place on greased baking sheet. Bake for 15–20 minutes or until lightly browned and firm to the touch. Cool on a wire rack.

Melt 2 tbsp. butter and whisk with the powdered sugar, coffee, and vanilla. (Glaze should be thick and opaque, coating the scones and retaining its café au lait color.) Drizzle scones with the glaze and serve with your favorite energy-packed beverage!

ESPRESSO YOURSELF!

You've just learned that your opportunities are unique to you as you serve others with the combination of your personality and gifts. Having explored this, discuss how the compilation of gifts in your small group can be put to use as you "Espresso Yourself!" through service together, pointing people to Christ as you do! Create and organize an event to benefit a group within your community, your church, a school, or a neighborhood. Examples include:

• An after-school event for children or youth, complete with snacks and activities,

• Neighborhood Christmas caroling with cookie trays to give away,

• *Sip, Savor, and Drink Deeply* women's event, complete with coffee, scones, and a devotion or Bible study,

• A 5K fun run or walk to promote wellness in the community, and

• An Easter (or other holiday) party for residents of a care facility.

Prayerfully consider how each person in your group can contribute her Specialty Blend of gifts toward the event. Some will utilize their strengths in organization, planning, and promotion. Others can contribute by adding creative touches and making gifts for the recipients. Others can make and serve food for the special event. Still others may lead by speaking, performing music, or planning group activities.

Whatever you do, **"Serve by the strength that God supplies— in order that in everything God may be glorified through Jesus Christ"** (1 Peter 4:11).

SIP, SAVOR, AND DRINK DEEPLY

MY OVERFLOWING CUP!

Coffee Break!
Check all that apply to you, and discuss as a group:

☐ My cup contains a unique specialty blend that equips me for the opportunities God has in store. (Share a drop of knowledge gained from the last session and have a memory-verse moment.)

☐ I hope my hot chocolate comes with (circle one or more): marshmallows, whipped cream, sprinkles.

☐ I like a little coffee with my cream, so I might as well order a breve.

☐ My creamy cappuccino provides calming comfort—until the caffeine kicks in!

☐ I love to (circle one or both) give/receive coffee-themed gifts!

_|_ **Memory Verse:** "May the God of hope fill you with all joy and peace in believing, so that by the power of the Holy Spirit you may abound [overflow] in hope." Romans 15:13

MY OVERFLOWING CUP

The announcement came across the intercom for all to hear: "Overflow! Cleanup needed near the coffee counter." A customer standing at the in-store coffee shop had a mishap. As I poked my head out of aisle six, I saw two employees walking swiftly toward the coffee counter, mop bucket in tow. The barista had filled the customer's cup to overflowing and a portion of its precious contents had spilled onto the floor.

When we hear "overflow," we may think, *Oh no! Something's been spilled!* as I had that day at the store. But when God fills us to overflowing, there is nothing accidental about it. Nothing is spilled or wasted. Overflowing speaks of plenty, abundance, and "beyond measure." (It cannot be measured and has no limit.) In the original Greek text of the New Testament, "abundance" and "overflow" were different forms of the very same word. They're synonymous. So picture the "spill," if you will, that happens only on purpose, the overflow that spills and splashes onto others and enables them to become drenched in God's abundance and grace because it has overflowed out of us, *by the Holy Spirit's power.*

HE FILLS YOUR CUP

We have talked about the power of the Holy Spirit across every session. The Third Person of the Trinity works mightily through God's Word AND through you because the Spirit *lives in you.*

a. Read **1 Corinthians 6:19**. In previous sessions, you've learned that you are likened to a "cup"—a vessel or clay jar—containing treasure. To what are you compared in this verse, and (begging the question) what do you contain, or "house"?

b. Revisit **Ephesians 3:16–17**, read earlier. Again, what do you house "in your inner being" because God has granted it to you? And what do you receive as a result?

c. Read **Romans 8:11**. Since it's true that the Holy Spirit dwells in you, what amazing ultimate thing do you receive, by His grace?

Just as God the Holy Spirit produced faith in you, so the Spirit continues to fill you . . . with the desire to study the Word and grow in Christ, and with courage and strength to share your faith. And it is by the power of the Holy Spirit that your cup *overflows* with every delicious thing, spilling and splashing onto others!

TAKE A SIP! You've received a specific taste of God's overflowing supply in each session, as you explored one of the countless items on The Savior's Grace Place Menu! Before we take a look at even more, review the first six menu items, writing them here and pausing to consider how the overflow of each may splash onto someone else today.

1. _____

2. _____

3. _____

4. _____

5. _____

6. _____

Mmm . . . what else do we see on this amazing menu?

THE SAVIOR'S GRACE PLACE MENU

7. Hot Chocolate Hope

The Savior's Grace Place Menu could not be complete without Hot Chocolate Hope—rich and creamy, overflowing with whipped cream, chocolate shavings, and sprinkles, and now available in gourmet flavors. Yum! Hot chocolate brings a smile to our faces. Hope does that . . . and so much more.

Our hope in Christ cannot be confused with the hope that's defined as merely "wishful thinking," like "I hope there's real whipped cream for my hot chocolate. I hope they have my favorite gourmet flavor." Real hope is a sweet gift in the Savior. **"According** to [God's] great mercy, He has caused us to be born again to a living hope through the resurrection of Jesus Christ from the dead" (1 Peter 1:3). In Jesus, our living hope is real and certain. God handed us hope in the manger, and He secured our hope at the cross and the empty tomb. We have the hope of salvation and eternal life in Christ. His resurrection—and the promise of the final resurrection for all who believe—is a reality, not wishful thinking. Now *that* brings a smile to my face . . . and joy and peace to my heart!

HOPE FOR TODAY

"May the God of hope fill you with all joy and peace in believing, so that by the power of the Holy Spirit you may abound [overflow] in hope" (Romans 15:13). The God of hope fills us with joy and peace through faith. We overflow with the hope He has poured into us by the Spirit's power. This hope enables us to get through the pain and difficulty that all too often fill our days. Maybe you have survived a disease, suffered from depression, or mourned a loss. Romans 5:3–4 says, "We rejoice in our sufferings, knowing that suffering produces endurance, and endurance produces character, and character produces hope." God can bring good out of our suffering. As He enables us to endure it, He produces character in us—the kind of character that allows us to empathize with others as they face similar sufferings because we have been there. And character produces hope—real hope in a real Savior who knows our needs and enables us to hang on to hope when sufferings abound because He promises that one day, He will deliver us out of them and into His arms. "Let us hold fast the confession of our hope without wavering, for He who promised is faithful" (Hebrews 10:23). We hold fast to our hope in Him, by His grace. And we hand out hope in His name. We point people to the Hope that IS Christ.

A few years ago, I lost my little sister, who had suffered with severe special needs. As my family and I walked through that time of grief together, one bright, shining truth pierced through the darkness of death: **hope**, the hope that we have in our Savior, Jesus, who has promised us that our loved ones who die in the faith are at rest with Him. They are free from the sufferings of this life and are home with their Savior. As my parents said good-bye to their daughter and as loved ones sought to console them, I heard my mom and my dad respond again and again, "She's with Jesus." This is the hope you and I have; it's the hope to which we point other people. One day, we, too, will be with Jesus. And there is more! We have Christ's promise that He will return again. With hope, we *await the final resurrection—the Day of Jesus Christ—when we will receive imperishable, glorious bodies like His:* **"Our citizenship is in heaven, and from it we await a Savior, the Lord Jesus Christ, who will transform our lowly body to be like His glorious body"** (Philippians 3:20–21). He will take us to heaven where we will live forever in the Father's house.

Jesus spoke of the Father's house, providing a peek into the promise of the final resurrection. It was the night before His crucifixion, just after He had finished the Passover meal with His disciples, and He was preparing them for the events that were about to take place. They were deeply troubled, and Jesus comforted them with His words.

HE FILLS YOUR CUP

Read the descriptive words of **John 14:1–7**, which contain Jesus' comforting promise about the Father's house and the way to get there. He is now preparing a place for you, and He promises to return and take you there.

a. You know the way to the Father's house already. What is it? How do you envision life in the Father's house, your place of permanent residence with your Savior? (See **Revelation 21:3–4** for a brief description. For further study, see **Revelation 21–22** to read about John's vision of our eternal dwelling place.)

b.   Where else does Jesus speak of His Father's house? See **Luke 2:49** and **John 2:16**. How are they the same? different?

c. Jesus said, **"I and the Father are one"** (John 10:30). To believe in the Father IS to believe in the Son. How do Jesus' words in **John 14:7** relate to those in **Colossians 1:15**?

HE FILLS YOUR CUP 3

1 Corinthians 15 provides great detail about Christ's resurrection and the hope of the final resurrection on the Day of Jesus Christ for all who believe in Him. Turn to **1 Corinthians 15:51–57** to read about this mystery, revealed!

a. What is meant by **"We shall not all sleep, but we shall all be changed"** (v. 51)?

b. In your own words, explain how **"Death is swallowed up in victory"** (v. 54). Describe the hope this passage gives you today.

With certain hope of victory in the final resurrection, we receive joy and peace today as we live our lives in light of eternity.

8. Cappuccino Comfort
"Blessed be the God and Father of our Lord Jesus Christ, the Father of mercies and God of all comfort, who comforts us in all

our affliction, so that we may be able to comfort those who are in any affliction, with the comfort with which we ourselves are comforted by God" (2 Corinthians 1:3–4).

You have heard of comfort food, right? How about a comfort drink? I'd like to introduce you to Cappuccino Comfort, the comforting beverage of choice on The Savior's Grace Place Menu. Sitting down to sip a steamy, creamy cappuccino, I am instantly calmed and comforted—that is, until the caffeine kicks in! The ever-popular cappuccino is an espresso topped with foamed, frothed milk, and it may include a pump or two of flavored syrup.

> [**Fresh-Brewed Fun Fact:** *Cappuccino* means "little cap," and traditionally, the foam topping was shaped to form a "cap" on the cappuccino; then it was dusted with spice or chocolate powder. When the cappuccino was first introduced in Italy, it was named after the Capuchin monks because of the similar brown color of their robes, complete with hoods called "cappuccios."]

Cappuccino Comfort came to me through my dear mentor, Marian, who called one day to suggest we meet for coffee. I was burdened with some difficulties and jumped at the opportunity to meet, knowing that time spent with Marian around a cup was like a soothing balm for my soul. I ordered my foam-capped French vanilla cappuccino, then sat next to my wise friend. As I poured out my problems, I sipped from my cup of liquid comfort and she listened. Marian responded with stories, some from decades past and others from the present, but all from the heart of a woman who had received unending comfort from God, even in the midst of her most difficult trials. God worked through Marian that day to comfort me with the same comfort He had given her countless times throughout her long life. She reminded me that He is truly "the Father of mercies and God of all comfort" who sent His Son to pardon me for my countless sins and pour out His comfort upon me in every difficult circumstance.

My creamy cappuccino filled me with a warm comfort of sorts, capped off with a *good word* of comfort from my mentor. The ultimate Comforter fills me with lasting comfort in His *good Word,* so I can comfort others just as Marian comforted me. God has poured out His comfort upon you, that you may comfort those He leads you to today.

TAKE A SIP! The God of all comfort pours out His comfort upon you. To whom is He leading you today, that you, too, may offer some Cappuccino Comfort?

HE FILLS YOUR CUP 4

Try another study approach as you read this collection of comforting verses, using the acronym **WORD**:

Word—Read God's *Word,* of course!

Observe—What do you *observe* in these passages and learn from them? (How does God comfort His people? When? With what does He comfort them? Other observations?)

Reflect and **R**elate—*Reflect* upon the messages and *relate* (apply) them to your life. (How and when have you received comfort from God? How do these truths speak to you today? Other reflections?)

Discuss—*Discuss* your observations and reflections with another person or as a group.

Psalm 23:4   2 Thessalonians 2:16–17
Psalm 119:76   Psalm 119:50
Isaiah 49:13

9. Breve Blessings!

A breve is perhaps the least-known beverage on a coffee shop menu. This delicious drink is created simply by substituting half-and-half or light cream for the milk in any espresso-based beverage. Take your latte, cappuccino, or mocha and simply replace the steamed milk with a creamier option and—voilà!—you have a breve. If you're thinking, *But I've always added cream to my coffee,* keep in mind that a breve is more parts *cream* than coffee. It's really rich!

We are brimming with God's Breve Blessings, overflowing for us in Christ and found on The Savior's Grace Place Menu! His blessings are not limited to the past. *(Sigh. My cup was rich and running over at one time.)* They're not restricted to special moments and milestone events we log in our memory books. In our sin, we are shortsighted. Not only do we fail to remember or recognize some of our blessings, but we also neglect to acknowledge and praise our Savior as the one who provides each and every one of them. We bring our shortsightedness and neglect to the Provider Himself, who knows our failures and forgives all of them for Jesus' sake, blessing us **"with every spiritual blessing"** (Ephesians 1:3), beginning with the forgiveness we receive at the cross and flowing forward with the blessings of faith, peace, love, joy, and more!

Today's blessings that fill our cups may have a new look, a different flavor than yesterday's blend, and we may not yet recognize them to be the blessings that they are. Maybe they'll appear through new means, revealing God's continued provision in a different way.

TAKE A SIP! Ask God to help you recognize your most recent blessings. Log them on page 113 (as in a memory book). Then take a moment to praise the Provider of every one of them!

One day, while waiting in line at my local coffee shop, I was startled as a woman appeared suddenly and grabbed me by the arm. With a smile larger than my grande breve, she exclaimed, "Can I pay for your drink? I am so blessed today, I just want to share my joy!" By God's grace, this woman recognized His rich blessings in her life and let them overflow onto me.

Praise be to God, our cups of Breve Blessings are brimming over! The Lord's blessings really do spill over from our cups of plenty; it's a never-ending flow.

HE FILLS YOUR CUP 5

God is the giver of every good and perfect gift—every blessing—both physical and spiritual, as we discussed in the last session. All that we have comes from His hand. Read **Ephesians 1:3–14**, which begins, "Blessed be the God and Father of our Lord Jesus Christ." We "bless" or *praise* our triune God—the Father, the Son, and the Holy Spirit—for His countless blessings, beginning with the spiritual blessings in Christ we read about here.

a. According to **verse 3**, you are blessed *in Christ*. Find and mark every "in Christ" or "in Him" across this passage. Why is "in Christ" so significant?

b. Because you are "in Christ," united with Him in your Baptism, you are a recipient of every spiritual blessing from heaven. Read the passage again, looking for some of the countless spiritual blessings you receive by His grace.

c. According to **verse 6**, the blessings you receive "in the Beloved"—in Christ, the one He loves—are the result of what?

Your cup truly does overflow with every spiritual blessing in Christ Jesus. Take a line-by-line look at the beloved **Psalm 23**, where King David penned the words "my cup overflows" (v. 5). What word or phrase comes to mind for each line of this psalm (below), as you reflect on God's perfect provision in your life? (For example, "The LORD is my shepherd" makes me think of the saving *relationship* I have with my Shepherd because of His grace for me in Christ.)

1 The LORD is my shepherd; _____

  I shall not want. _____

2 He makes me lie down in green pastures. _____

  He leads me beside still waters. _____

3 He restores my soul. _____

  He leads me in paths of righteousness _____

  for His name's sake. _____

4 Even though I walk through the valley of the shadow of death, _____

  I will fear no evil, _____

  for You are with me; _____

  Your rod and Your staff, they comfort me. _____

5 You prepare a table before me in the presence of my enemies;

  _____

  You anoint my head with oil; _____

  my cup overflows. _____

6 Surely goodness and mercy shall follow me all the days of my life, _____

  and I shall dwell in the house of the LORD forever.

  _____

Pull up a chair and settle in. God offers you the entire menu—all this and more—today and every day. Receive refreshment and delight for your soul! Drink deeply as your cup continues to overflow.

The psalmist says, **"I will lift up the cup of salvation and call on the name of the LORD"** (Psalm 116:13). By His grace, God has given me this cup of salvation—eternal life—in Christ. I lift it up in thanksgiving for His great gift. By the mighty Spirit's power, I praise His holy name!

My cup overflows . . .

Prayer

God of hope, I praise You for the hope of salvation that's secured for me in Christ! Enable me to hold fast to hope during difficulties, because You are faithful. I praise and thank You for Your comfort in all my afflictions. Lead me to offer the same comfort to someone else who struggles, as I remind them of Your eternal comfort and good hope through grace in Christ. Help me to recognize Your rich blessings as they flow into my life, sometimes through unexpected means. May I give You glory as I acknowledge and praise You for each and every one. My cup overflows! In Jesus' name. Amen.

Cappuccino Shortbread Cookies

Savor and share this special cookie containing the ultimate comfort food AND comfort drink! Dipped in chocolate, this cappuccino cookie is the perfect side to your cup of liquid comfort.

Shortbread

⅔ c. butter, softened

½ tsp. vanilla

1¼ c. flour

½ c. powdered sugar

2 tsp. instant espresso or coffee granules

Chocolate Glaze

1 c. (8 oz.) mini semisweet chocolate morsels

1 tsp. coconut oil

Preheat oven to 325°. Cream butter and vanilla together; slowly stir in flour, sugar, and coffee granules. Roll dough between sheets of parchment or waxed paper until it is approximately ½ inch thick. Cut into circles. Place cookies on a parchment-lined cookie sheet. Bake for 20–25 minutes until lightly browned and firm. Let shortbread cool completely. Place chocolate chips and coconut oil in a microwave-proof bowl. Heat on High for 30 seconds; stir well, and then heat in 10-second increments, stirring well between each heating, until completely melted. Dip half of each cookie into the chocolate and place on a wire rack to firm up.

ESPRESSO YOURSELF!

Filled to the brim with hope, comfort, and blessings, your group gathers one last time to "Espresso Yourself!" together! How can you serve others from the overflow as you express your hope in Christ with them? To whom can you offer comfort? How can you bless them as you consider your blessings too numerous to count?

Maybe there's a special woman or a family for whom your group has been praying. Assemble a giant gift basket filled with an assortment of items that will bless your recipient(s) and serve as a tangible reminder of the hope and comfort that you'd like to share with them. Maybe your basket can overflow with a combination of gifts: (1) some of the gifts you've created throughout this study (like a memory mug, latte mix, coffee candle decor, and lip scrub); (2) a few of the coffee-themed recipes you've made (candies, cookies, and biscotti), packaged in cellophane or tins; (3) a collection of coffee-themed gift items, such as: coffee novelties and decor, flavored coffees, gift cards to a coffee shop, a collection of handwritten coffee-themed recipes, a set of cup coasters, a bottle of flavored coffee syrup, and a *Sip, Savor, and Drink Deeply* devotional.

Gather selected items, including those you made during previous "Espresso Yourself!" sessions. Personalize items for your recipient. Which Scripture verses might you select as you consider the specific encouragement you'd like to provide? What kinds of labels or personal notes can you create for some of the gift items before you tuck them into the basket? Arrange a time that your group can hand-deliver this basket full of blessings, and pray for your recipient on the way!

"HE FILLS YOUR CUP" ANSWERS

SESSION 1

1 a. Cleaning the inside would mean acknowledging and confessing sin (their greed, self-indulgence, and more) that permeated them from within. The religious leaders were giving lip service to their man-made laws and high regard for the many traditions and religious observances they held dear, thus providing the outward appearance of being clean. All the while, they ignored the heart and its struggle with sin—the need for repentance. Only Christ can cleanse a person of their sins—and He does so from the inside out!

    b. Their man-made religious observances included ceremonial ritual washing of everything from hands to cups, from other cooking utensils to furniture, all for ceremonial cleanliness. Jesus could effectively use the cup metaphorically to speak of their vain attempts to outwardly cleanse themselves by their works, and contrast that with true cleansing through forgiveness received by faith in Christ.

2 a. He was referring to the cup of ultimate suffering. If the cup was passed from Him, He would be spared crucifixion and death, but we would not have a Savior. Drinking it meant He would suffer for the sins of the whole world—for you and me—upon the cross, providing forgiveness for our sins and salvation in His name.

    b. Out of His love for us, the sinless Son of God yields perfectly to the Father's will, even though it means suffering for Him. At the same time, the Son of Man suffers deep anguish, crying out to the Father, knowing His "cup" contains the torture and crucifixion that lies ahead.

3. You may choose to take turns reading aloud the prayer in Psalm 51; discuss words or phrases that stand out to each person. Silently reflect on a sin you wish to confess to Jesus. Then turn your pen or pencil upside-down and write invisibly a confession you struggle with, knowing that your confession is not invisible to Jesus. He sees, forgives, cleanses, and strengthens. Remind one another of Christ's power and promise to forgive.

4. Wording will vary, but may include: God has fearfully and wonderfully made me (Psalm 139:14); I am His workmanship, created in Christ for the purposes He prepared in advance for me (Ephesians 2:10)! He loves me so much, He calls me His child (1 John 3:1), and nothing in all creation can ever separate me from His love for me in Christ Jesus (Romans 8:38–39). I am solely defined by God's everlasting love for me (Jeremiah 31:3)!

5 a. I am as clay, the work of God's hand; I am being fashioned according to His design (Isaiah 64:8). I am a vessel, an instrument that is useful to the Master and ready for every good work (2 Timothy 2:21). I am a jar of clay—an earthen vessel—that carries the treasure of the Gospel (2 Corinthians 4:7).

b. We contain and carry the greatest treasure in the world. We are merely the vessels chosen to hold and to deliver the treasure of the Gospel. As Paul says in verse 5, "What we proclaim is not ourselves, but Jesus Christ as Lord." We carry the message of Christ, crucified and risen! The power of the Gospel belongs to God; He brings a person to faith; we simply share it. We point others to the priceless treasure and not to the jar of clay.

6. Wording will vary. He traded His perfect riches to become the poorest of the poor, taking on the sins of the world and receiving the curse of death that comes with sin. He took our punishment and our place at the cross, and we in turn receive the riches of His grace, the forgiveness of sins, and eternal life in Him.

SESSION 2

1. Illustrations will vary. Perhaps some of the words can flow downward toward the image of a heart.

2 a. He fills us with compassion (Isaiah 49:13) and comfort (Isaiah 49:13; 2 Corinthians 1:3–4), generosity (2 Corinthians 9:11), wisdom (James 1:5), strength (Isaiah 40:28–31), and the ability to forgive (Ephesians 4:32) and to love as He first loved us (1 John 4:19).

b. Provide index cards or sticky notes and encourage one another to choose and write a selected verse, honoring confidentiality as women attach names to the verses and tuck away their reminder notes.

c. Answers will vary. Needs may include those read in the verses, but they may also include many others, like peace, joy, contentment, grace, and more. Use a Bible concordance or a word search on a Bible app or website to find verses where God speaks to these needs.

3. Answers will vary, but may include the peace and comfort we receive knowing that God will provide for every need that comes our way, viewing our needs in light of eternity.

4 a. In both, God is acting on our behalf according to His riches in glory. All of God's riches are ours because of Christ's sacrifice for us at the cross. In Philippians 4:19, He speaks of supplying every need we have; in Ephesians 3:16, He speaks of supplying strength through the Holy Spirit.

b. Chosen words will be unique to each person. Allow time for everyone to contemplate the extent of Christ's love. Fully God, Christ fulfilled our greatest need: a Savior! All the fullness of God dwells in Christ (Colossians 1:19). Though we cannot fully grasp the extent of God's limitless love in Christ, we receive the full measure of it! Our cups overflow.

c. *Far more abundantly.* Beyond our wildest imagination, God works in and through us in amazing ways!

5. Answers will vary but may include: asking for a teachable heart (Psalm 25:5); needing the reminder to sip slowly—to "open [my] mouth wide and [He] will fill it" (Psalm 81:10); to meditate on God's Word and the message He has for me today; beginning my refill time with great expectations that the Holy Spirit will work powerfully (2 Peter 1:3).

6. As time allows, sift through the pages of 1 John together, helping one another locate the word *love* as it appears on the pages. Read a few of the verses aloud as you do.

SESSION 3

1. Include a quiet moment for personal prayer as each person has the opportunity to confess her struggles and pray for strength, bravery, a way of escape, and more. Discuss or pray aloud, as the group feels comfortable.

2 a. Words or phrases chosen will vary. Seek the Lord; seek His strength; seek His presence (1 Chronicles 16:11); equipped me with strength; made my way blameless (Psalm 18:32); strength; song; salvation (Psalm 118:14); Your Word; lamp to my feet; light to my path (Psalm 119:105); hear a word; this is the way, walk in it (Isaiah 30:21); I know the plans I have for you; plans for welfare and not for evil; future; hope (Jeremiah 29:11); strong in the Lord; strength of His might; armor of God; stand against

the accusations and schemes of the devil (Ephesians 6:10–11).

b. Answers will vary but may include: We can spill the beans in our Savior's strength as we seek His presence. He will equip us with His strength as He shows us His way (His path for us) in His Word. He will tell us the way we should walk, guiding our steps. He knows His plans for us, to give us a hope and a future. He gives us His armor; in His strength, we can stand against the schemes of Satan.

c. Answers will vary but may include: Following God's lead and seeking His strength to make a change brings honor to Him. Someone near us may be impacted for Christ as he or she witnesses our reliance on God's Word and His strength. (Encourage discussion.)

3. We are weak on our own, but His power rests on us! Though God's power is already perfect, it is made more obvious and evident in our weakness as we humbly admit our need for His strength and submit to Him. As we surrender our every weakness to Him, not only does His grace cover us, but we can also be assured in the midst of temptation that His power is what gives us strength to stand up under it.

4. Answers will vary but may include: Heavenly treasures have eternal value; filling my heart with them rather than with temporal earthly treasures, I'm truly satisfied (Matthew 6:19–21). I need God's help to "turn my eyes from looking at worthless things" (Psalm 119:37), and I don't want to be dominated or controlled by anything that's not beneficial to me (1 Corinthians 6:12). I must guard my heart and keep it "with all vigilance" (Proverbs 4:23), alert and attentive to discern what's coming my way before I allow it to fill my cup. (Addressing each question and living out the answers will be unique to each person. Encourage writing down specific ideas that can serve as goals, supported and sustained in Christ.)

5. Answers will vary but may include: His grace overflows for me in Christ (1 Timothy 1:14)! As I consume His Word, I know that I'll continue to be filled beyond measure, by the power of the Spirit. I can enter God's house for worship, "kneel[ing] before the Lord, our Maker" (Psalm 95:6), knowing that I'll receive His Means of Grace there; once again, my cup overflows! And I can seek out brothers and sisters in Christ for support and encouragement, as we "stir up one another to love and good works" (Hebrews 10:24).

6. We should be anxious about nothing and praying about everything! He desires that we bring every prayer and supplication—every request—to

Him. God wants to hear every concern we have as we bring it to Him in faith. As we lay our requests, anxieties, and prayers before Him, He trades them for His peace in Christ. The peace we receive is beyond our comprehension!

SESSION 4

1 a. Jesus warns against covetousness (greed or envy over another person's material things). Our lives should not find their focus or fulfillment in the vast quantity "abundance" of our possessions.

b. Real abundance is found in God's provision and mercy in Christ; our lives are abundantly full and complete in the One who came to give us life (John 10:10). In sharp contrast, life is not made up of the abundance of possessions, which may lead to covetousness and sin (Luke 12:15).

c. The love of money is a root of evil. Wording will vary, but may include: The love of money is like a root that grows all kinds of evil thoughts and practices. It may lead people to stray from their faith in Christ and they may end up hurting themselves as a result.

d. Answers will be unique to each person. Encourage discussion, but respect the silence of those who wish to keep their thoughts private.

2 a. Paul learned that he could be content in material plenty or want; his physical provision did not determine his contentment. First column: abound, plenty, abundance. Second column: brought low, hunger, need.

b. Paul can be content in every circumstance through the source and secret of His strength: Christ!

c. Answers will vary. Much discontent happens when a person's focus shifts from the Provider and to the provision, often because the provision is temporal and fleeting, unable to fulfill in the way that only the Provider can. Encourage one another to share examples from your lives.

d. Discussions will vary.

3. He provides in abundance: His goodness (Psalm 31:19), mercy (Psalm 69:16), steadfast love (Psalm 69:13), food/physical needs (Psalm 78:25), salvation, wisdom, knowledge (Isaiah 33:5–6), and pardon (Isaiah 55:7). Specific provision will be unique to each woman. Take time for individual or group prayer.

4. Answers will vary, but may include: R = READ (Read the passage together.) E = EXAMINE I learned more about God's incredible love for me in Christ. Through several rhetorical questions (Romans 8:31–35), the apostle Paul speaks of God's love in action through Christ's cross, and even includes a lengthy list of the many circumstances that unsuccessfully seek to separate me from His love (v. 35), followed by a tenfold list of supernatural threats that also fail to separate me from His all-encompassing love in Christ (vv. 38–39). A = APPLY Since God is for me, sent His Son to save me, and graciously gives me all I need, no one can condemn me. Jesus died, rose, and ascended into heaven where He intercedes for me every time I pray. He conquered death for me; I have victory and life in Him. No one and nothing can separate me from His love! P = PRAYER (Take time for prayer, using this passage as a guide.)

5. Bring your troubles to God's throne of grace. Choose Psalm 13 or another Psalm of Lament and pray together or individually through the psalm, receiving hope and healing in God's promises.

6. Perhaps assign the Bible verses listed to various individuals or small groups. Then tell them to, on your cue, shout together simultaneously their words of praise. Or, for fun, choose a hymn of praise and assign the various stanzas to be sung at the same time by individuals or small groups. Encourage one another to sing or shout without hesitation, as together you let your praises overflow from your lips.

SESSION 5

1. Answers will vary. Encourage one another to share and write/save selected verses to serve as reminders.

2. By faith, living water flows out of our hearts; we are filled to overflowing with the Holy Spirit. He invites us to come to Him to have our thirst quenched; He fills us as only He can.

3 a. Answers may include: In my sin, I fail to abide with Jesus and vainly attempt to bear fruit on my own, but I know that apart from Him, I can do nothing (John 15:4–5). I also fail to keep His commandments—to love others (vv. 10, 12). Confessing these sins to my Savior, I know that I am cleansed according to His Word (v. 3).

b. Answers may include: I learn that I am chosen in Christ, the True Vine (vv. 1, 16). He loves me just as the Father loves Him (v. 9). Because of His love for me, He prunes me so that I may bear more fruit (v. 2). He wants me to keep His commandments, abiding in His love (v. 10); His commandment is that I love others as He loves me (v. 12). Jesus calls me His friend (v. 14)! He reveals His Father's will to me (v. 15). As He has chosen me, He calls me to bear fruit that lasts (v. 16).

c. Answers will include specific praises and responses, but may include: I praise Him because He has chosen me (v. 16); He abides with me as a vine is connected to its branches (v. 5), and He loves me enough to prune me so I can be even more fruitful (v. 2). God is praised and glorified when I bear fruit in Jesus' name (v. 8). I respond by desiring that His words abide in me; I bring my requests to Him, trusting His will be done (v. 7). I want to bear fruit in every part of my life, following His command to love others (v. 12).

4. Specific application to relationships will be unique to each person, but general guidance from these verses may include the following: *Encouragement*—We are called to encourage and build up our friends (1 Thessalonians 5:11), exhorting (urging) them toward spiritual growth (Hebrews 3:13), and stirring them up to love and good works (Hebrews 10:24), edifying them as we grow alongside them in the Word and in prayer. Maybe we can find Scripture that applies to our friends' situations and help them apply it. *Accountability*—We are called to confront our friends (and vice versa) when caught in sin, forgiving them when they repent (Luke 17:3), gently restoring them with a loving warning and guiding them away from the sin (Galatians 6:1). *Grace*—We are called to bear with one another, to forgive our friends just as God has forgiven us (Colossians 3:13), extending His grace as we confess our sins to one another and pray for each other (James 5:16).

5. Our generosity toward others should be like that of God's grace for us: rich and running over! Our "boomerang blessing" comes as we receive with the same generosity we have given, but that should not be the motivation for giving. Personal examples will be unique to each person.

6. We have the "same spirit of faith" given to all believers of every generation; this faith springs forward into words and action, by the Spirit's power. Because we believe, we cannot help but speak of the faith that flows from us (2 Corinthians 4:13)! In Christ, we have life and breath and movement (Acts 17:28). By our words and the work of our hands, the world around us will know that He lives in us by faith.

1. Answers will vary as women respond in their own words, but may include: God, our Creator, provides every good gift we have (James 1:17), along with the purpose and strength to use them (1 Peter 4:11); He establishes our hearts in every good work (2 Thessalonians 2:17), for which we were uniquely created in Christ (Ephesians 2:10)! It is He who works in us, according to His will and purpose (Philippians 2:13), as we use our gifts to serve others and to glorify God in Christ (1 Peter 4:10–11).

2. Romans 12 gift list: prophecy, service, teaching, exhortation/encouragement, giving/contributing, leading, showing mercy. Encourage discussion regarding which gift(s) each of you recognizes as your own, as well as those you see in one another through the use of them.

3 a. You can give your best effort, working "heartily"—with the same wholeheartedness you would have if you were working directly for the Lord.

b. Ultimately, you are serving Jesus, and your reward is your inheritance in heaven, received not by your works but by faith in the one you serve.

c. Remembering your real reward and who you serve can help you give your best and persevere in the midst of difficult or unfair service.

4. Each creative expression will look as unique as the person drawing it! God makes ALL grace abound to us, therefore, giving us ALL sufficiency in ALL things at ALL times. The result? We are able to abound (overflow) in every good work! (Encourage one another to list unique opportunities overflowing from your cups.)

5. You are enriched by God with every good gift, beginning with His abundant grace and including your Specialty Blend of talents and traits, so that you may serve others generously and give thanks to God! He may be using you to (1) supply the very needs of His people and (2) lead them to lives overflowing with thanks and praise.

6 a. Honor Christ in your heart, growing in Him through worship and through the study of His Word; it's there that He prepares you, through the Spirit's power, to have a ready answer for "anyone who asks you for a reason for the hope that is in you" (1 Peter 3:15). Seek His wisdom for every decision, through His Word, and in prayer (James 1:5).

b. Answers will vary but may include: We can know that He works His energy within us because we have His Word on it (Colossians 1:29)! As we seek His wisdom and follow His lead, we also trust His promise that He works in us "to will and to work" (desire and act) according to His purpose (Philippians 2:13).

SESSION 7

1 a. Your body is a temple, the very vessel that houses the Holy Spirit!

  b. You house the Holy Spirit. You receive strength with the Spirit's power, and faith in Christ, who dwells in you.

  c. Life eternal in Christ! Just as He was resurrected from the dead, so your mortal body will be raised too!

2 a. Jesus is the way—the only way—to the Father's house. Encourage one another to share how you envision the Father's heavenly home that Jesus prepares for us, the place where there will be no more death, mourning, crying, or pain. (See Revelation 21 and 22.)

  b. Jesus' first recorded words in Scripture are from His Father's house as a boy (Luke 2:49). It was also His Father's house where He turned over the money-changers' tables (John 2:16). The earthly temple was the temporary dwelling place of God where His people could approach Him in a limited sense. In Christ, we are God's temple because His Spirit dwells in us (1 Corinthians 3:16)! We will dwell with God fully and forever in His heavenly house!

  c. To know Jesus is to know the Father. Jesus says, "You do know Him and have seen Him" (John 14:7), because Jesus is "the image of the invisible God" (Colossians 1:15).

3 a. Many believers have fallen asleep in the Lord, but some will still be alive when Christ returns. The dead will rise and all believers will be changed. In an instant, all will trade mortal, perishable bodies for immortal, imperishable bodies (1 Corinthians 15:51–53).

  b. Wording will vary, but may include: The Law reveals our sin, which leads to death. Christ fulfilled the Law for us at the cross, taking on our sin. His victorious resurrection, which swallowed up death, is our victory! We have eternal life in Him!

4. W = WORD (Take turns reading the verses aloud.) O = OBSERVE God comforts His people with His presence, using His "rod and staff" (His guidance, direction, and discipline) for His people's protection (Psalm 23:4); He comforts with the promise of His love (Psalm 119:76), and with compassion (Isaiah 49:13); by His grace, He comforts His people's hearts with an eternal comfort through the hope He has given in Christ (2 Thessalonians 2:16–17); and He comforts His people through His promise that gives life (Psalm 119:50). R = REFLECT Answers will vary and may include stories of receiving God's comfort, but may include, in general: God is my ultimate source of comfort! I receive God's comfort in all my afflictions. I am comforted, knowing He is always with me, He guides and protects me, He loves me, and He has given me eternal comfort through the certain hope of salvation I have in Christ. D = DISCUSS (Enjoy rich discussion, encouraging each person to share her observations and personal reflections.)

5 a. (These phrases occur in verses 3, 4, 6 [in the Beloved], 7, 9, 10, 11, 12, 13 [twice].) God chose us in Christ, through whom we have the forgiveness of our sins; we have the inheritance of heaven! Our blessings come through the One who gives us life and salvation. We are reconciled to the Father through Christ, and because all who are baptized are "in Christ," we are reconciled to them as well.

b. We receive the blessings of: being chosen in Christ (v. 4); being made holy and blameless before God through Christ's work at the cross (v. 4); adoption as God's children through Christ (v. 5); redemption, forgiveness, and grace (v. 7); knowing the mystery of His will, which was fulfilled in Christ (v. 9); receiving an inheritance (v. 11); faith by the power of the Holy Spirit, through the hearing of the Gospel (v. 13).

c. The blessings we receive are the result of God's grace, not something we earn or deserve.

6. Words or phrases will vary. Suggestions: verse 1—relationship; supply and provision; verse 2—rest; refreshment; verse 3—healing and peace; guidance and righteousness; purpose; verse 4—trial; protection; faithfulness and presence; discipline and comfort; verse 5—provision and protection; blessings; abundance; verse 6—grace and mercy and God's goodness; hope and salvation.

SIP, SAVOR, AND DRINK DEEPLY